Easy to love

Easy to love

SOUTHERN STORIES
FROM THE HEART

—

To Phil & Ann,
Enjoy reading about
the folks from Carrollton.

Joe Garrett

ISBN: 1535549610
ISBN 13: 9781535549615
Library of Congress Control Number: 2016915896
CreateSpace Independent Publishing Platform
North Charleston, South Carolina

Author's Note: some essays have been edited slightly by the author since their original publication.

For my wife, Ali, and my sons, Turner, Charlie, and Henry

In loving memory of my son Will

Will Garrett, Ft. Lauderdale 2012

CONTENTS

INTRODUCTION
by
Mike Steed

———

A story has no beginning or end: arbitrarily one
chooses that moment of experience of which to
look back or from which to look ahead.

—GRAHAM GREENE

L et me be subtle: buy this book. Don't share it. It's not sanitary to share books, and it may prevent people from having it for themselves and getting a copy for everyone on their gift lists.

I love good writers, and Joe Garrett is a good writer. He has compiled some of his best work in the volume you hold in your hands right now. A good writer can construct sentences, tie them together in some manner of coherence to form a paragraph, and more, as you will see in *Easy to Love.*

Joe spent his college days studying journalism at the most noble of institutions, the University of Georgia. He was apprenticed to Dan Magill as a student assistant. No Bulldog has to be reminded of Magill, the legendary sports information director and tennis coach. He had a syrupy southern accent that was heard for years and years on so many football broadcasts. He was known by his voice just as quickly as Larry Munson. He was a repository of UGA sports history, lore, philosophy, and lessons for life. Garrett tells us more about Magill, one of his most prominent mentors. I expect that Magill explained to Joe that "Go Dawgs" is a complete sentence containing both a noun and a verb.

Another trait of a good writer is being a reader. Throughout this collection you find evidence to support how much Joe Garrett loves reading. His appetite for literature ranges from the Kathy Ireland swimsuit issue of *Sports Illustrated* to the works of Lewis Grizzard and Leo Tolstoy. (Can't believe I just used Grizzard and Tolstoy in the same sentence, now twice.) *Easy to Love* makes frequent use of a dialogue style and many quotations. Joe's timely, appropriate quotations from books, songs, and movies invariably amplify the point of his story.

A good writer is a good storyteller. To be a good storyteller, one must possess a way-better-than-average memory. Joe has that. He can paint word pictures that allow the reader to virtually taste a biscuit or a piece of cracklin' cornbread. He can remember the pranks and pleasures of coming of age in rural Georgia. He names names. He takes us to the front porch of a more gentle time.

The good writer has to be a keen observer of the human condition and, perhaps, more importantly, have lived through some experiences that define us mortals. The hard realities of life show up in Joe's words. His parents and family deal with the Alzheimer's of his mother. In the harshest, most profound experience imaginable, Joe and his wife, Ali, are living through one of life's greatest tragedies, the loss of their son, Will.

This book could not exist without poignant memories and heart twisting accounts of incredible grief that will never end. No doubt, writing about it has therapeutic value. As Joe informs us, one has to confront grief—stare it down—accept it as a part of life. Joe acknowledges, "There are no shortcuts through grief."

Ali and Joe might not agree they are examples of strength and grace, for they alone know their private times. But for the rest of us, they have, however unwillingly, become examples of looking forward. After all, they have Turner, Charlie, and Henry to shepherd through the joys, trials, and foibles of growing up. And they have each other.

Garrett has thoughtfully partitioned the book into Summer, Fall, Winter, and Spring—a big ol' metaphor for the seasons of the year and for our lives. Once you read the selected works included in each part, you will see how well you are led through this journey. In these pages you will find nostalgia, hilarity, nonsense, and exhilaration. You will experience hunger, joy, sadness, pain, pleasure, grief, redemption, and love. You will find inspiration emerging from despair. The reader is taken on a journey that is never dull.

Joe Garrett was raised right. He is blessed with wonderful parents, Jimmy and Betty. He loves his in-laws, the Turners. His grandparents make frequent appearances in the pages along with friends and ne'er-do-wells to season some of the stories. He adores his wife and cherishes his boys. We get to share some of that in the adventures presented here.

It has been my good fortune to know some good writers over my rather lengthy span of years. I've spent time with Lewis Grizzard, Chuck Perry, Ferrol Sams, Pat Conroy, Jim Minter, Bill Emerson, and my dear late brother, Bob Steed. There are more I could add like Keith Dunavant, Margaret Ann Barnes, and some I have met and admire like Joe Cumming. I will quickly add Joe Garrett to my list.

In a time when printed newspapers are folding like a cheap beach chair, Joe, like Lewis Grizzard and Dave Barry, gives us a reason to buy one. His words inspire us to "pause and reflect" so we can "keep moving." His general interest columns in *Times-Georgian* of Carrollton, Georgia, wisely avoid the acrimonious politics of the day. His style reels you in from the first, crisp lead lines of his essays and delivers you to the place he intended at the end.

John Barrymore said, "Happiness often sneaks in through a door you didn't know you left open." Joe Garrett, in spite of the grief visited upon him, has left a door open for us with his book, *Easy to Love.*

PART I

SUMMER

———

It's not the song we remember so fondly. It's
the memory the song brings to us.

—MIKE LIVELY

A SUMMER RIDE

West Georgia Living, June, 2014

———

Blame it on the Barney Gray Motel.

Before the final school bells rang to start summer vacation, my mom filled our wood-paneled station wagon with suitcases, a cooler full of NuGrape sodas, homemade sugar cookies, and enough parched peanuts to devour until we reached the Georgia state line.

Looking back, the five-hour ride staring out the windshield at the farmlands along the Alabama and Florida countryside occupied our time with enthusiasm. We always smiled when my dad stopped along Highway 231 to exchange a few dollars with an old man wearing faded Liberty overalls pawning watermelons from the flatbed of an old Ford. It meant I could finally quit asking my parents, "How much longer until we're there?"

Once again, the land of goofy golf courses, reptile farms, fried seafood, and tacky gift shops filled with shark teeth, seashells, and air-brushed T-shirts awaited our family's annual pilgrimage to the white, sandy beaches of Panama City Beach, Florida.

The Kennedys vacationed on Cape Cod along Nantucket Sound in Hyannis Port. The Bushes sought comfort in Kennebunkport. Even the great financial wizards J.P. Morgan and William Rockefeller found serenity on Jekyll Island.

As for my family, we seized refuge at the Barney Gray Motel.

By today's standards, the Barney Gray would qualify as run-down public housing at best—but in the early 1970s, we invaded the pool, shuffle board courts, and enjoyed floating in the ocean and building sandcastles at this seaside retreat.

One may argue the adventure of a vacation begins when we reach our destination. Maybe it's true in today's world, filled with safer cars, video consoles to watch movies, and hand-held iPads for entertainment. As for the vacations from my childhood, it was like strapping a saddle to a bull and riding.

We never wore seatbelts.

While my brothers occupied the middle row of the station wagon, I headquartered in the back, surrounded by our luggage. When boredom sunk in, we did what most boys liked to do: we wrestled, did backflips across the seats, and would even occasionally climb up front and stand in between my parents in the front row, while my mom held onto us.

We did all of this while dad drove the station wagon at sixty miles per hour.

Do you think my parents ever worried about our safety? No. And neither did anybody else's parents who passed us in their wood-paneled station wagons along the way. If my dad had to make a sudden stop, we would just brace ourselves as we fell out of our seats.

Thankfully, we never had a wreck.

Vacations were my favorite times of the year when I was a child. And they still are today.

I still eagerly await going places and long to return to the scent of the salty air, ocean waves, and the magnificent colors of the evening sky as the sun sets beyond the sea.

Vacations represent respite, relaxation, peace, and serenity to so many, but for me, it's really about family—and touching the depths within each of us to reflect what's really important.

"If you get the chance to travel—go," my friend Mike Lively wrote to me in a letter last year. "If you have a choice between sleeping in or getting up to see a fabulous sunrise, casting a fly rod on a babbling stream or walking on the beach, by all means—get up. There will ALWAYS be more than enough time to sleep."

Last year, I awakened before my family and walked to the beach before sunrise. For a moment, all that really mattered was watching darkness evolve into light to begin another day.

There were no worries, no deadlines and no bills to pay. All that really mattered was the moment, the now—and the opportunity to know there's something bigger in this world than our day-to-day journey. Thankfully, I discovered nature's marvelous gift.

It's amazing what one learns when he unbuckles his seatbelt.

Joe and dad Jimmy gulfside at the Barney Gray Motel in Panama City Beach, Florida 1974.

BUFORD PUSSER MEMORIAL FIELD

Times-Georgian, January 6, 2012

———

S he let us dig up her yard.

In all of the years that Carol Martin lived in the Chapel Heights subdivision in Carrollton, Georgia, she never won a beautification award for her lawn. Instead of planting flowers, she allowed the neighborhood kids to build a ball field in her front yard.

It was perfect for baseball in the summer and football in the fall.

She even adorned her front yard with a sign that read Buford T. Pusser Memorial Field, as named by some of the neighborhood kids as a tribute to Joe Don Baker's portrayal of a small town sheriff in their favorite movie, *Walking Tall.*

Although the sign is no longer around, and the field has been retired, the memories of playing in Carol's front yard are still alive.

How many kids do you see these days playing a pickup game of baseball without any parental supervision?

Carol and her husband Dr. Mac Martin's yard became more than a place for recreation—it was the best school I ever attended. My apologies to the writer Robert Fulghum, but everything I needed to know, I learned in Carol Martin's front yard.

It's not I don't like organized sports and activities. I just liked playing in her yard better than any recreation league.

We made our own games and rules.

And like members of the US Congress, we often debated and argued. Unlike today's political leaders, we would always come to an amicable agreement.

We pushed each other to become better. We laughed often. We sometimes fought and cried. But most of all, we had the best neighborhood team in the area, as nearby squads from Edgewood Drive, Sunset Hills, and the Southgate Neighborhood would often leave Chapel Heights in defeat.

Carol often walked out to say hello and even occasionally brought us lemonade. One time when we simply wanted to make the pitcher's mound bigger, we knocked on her door.

"Mrs. Martin, would you mind if we make a larger mound?" we asked.

"No," she replied. "The shovel is in the garage. Please make sure you put it back when you're finished."

I never saw her complain. Even when Dr. Martin arrived home from a long day at the hospital, he would often walk out on the field and say hello. He told me at Carol's funeral home visitation, "We absolutely loved watching all of you play in our yard."

Four years ago, Santa Claus delivered two miniature excavators to my sons for Christmas. When my boys started digging a big patch in our front yard, I immediately felt my blood pressure rise. It quickly lowered as I thought about Carol Martin's lawn.

When I told her this story, she replied, "Oh, let them tear up the yard. You'll have plenty of time to plant flowers and win a beautification award when they're grown."

I'm following her advice. I'm letting them dig.

Turner (left) and Will (right) at work in the back yard.

MAW MAW'S SKILLET

Southern Spice, *Times-Georgian,* July 15, 2012

———

I fell in love with fried okra at an early age.

Sunday lunches at my grandparents' house occupied a part of my summers as a child. Every spring, Paw Paw plowed his garden with a mule and grew a smorgasbord of vegetables. While he worked outside, Maw Maw snapped beans and shelled peas in the kitchen while she listened on her AM radio to an out-of-breath, sweaty preacher shout through the airwaves, "REPENT!"

This was long before the farm-to-table movement currently sweeping the country. No one had even heard of the words "organic" or "foodies." We ate "local" because everything from the squash to the cucumbers on our plates arrived straight from the garden.

My memory of these Sunday visits always returns when a sudden whiff fills my nostrils of hot grease while my wife simmers okra in an old, seasoned black iron skillet.

Summertime is my favorite food season of the year.

For the next few weeks, a red tomato, corn on the cob, green beans, cucumbers, and so many other vegetables will taste their best, but above all—I'll take my fried okra.

"I eat fried okra like popcorn this time of year," said my friend Jeff Gordon, operator of Big Daddy's Produce, as I purchased the edible green seed pods from him at Carrollton's Cotton Mill Farmers Market.

I've never really liked slimy boiled okra, but I also don't like fried okra from most restaurants. Most restaurants serve frozen okra with a breaded crust that doesn't actually stick to the okra—and that should be forbidden, especially in the South.

Okra should be dipped in flour or cornmeal and coat the little green vegetable when finished cooking. It's at its best when it's prepared at home.

Since Maw Maw died in 1996, I haven't eaten fried okra that tasted like hers. My mother, who fried scrumptious okra, could never make hers taste like Maw Maw's.

She missed something. And after all these years, I've figured out Maw Maw's secret ingredient—lard.

Mike Steed, international pig-fat epicure of Bowdon, published his not-so best-selling book *Cooking with Lard* the same year Maw Maw died. Although the book still remains banned by the "food police" in most health food stores, I predict one hundred years from now it will be regarded as a fried food classic.

"It is a fact that lard is the difference in the way things are and the way things used to be—at least as far as eating is concerned," Steed writes. "They (the 'food police') have taken nearly all the pleasure out of our sense of taste. The lack of lard is the big difference."

It's true the cooking world is moving towards spray cans of olive oil and an overall healthier way of eating, but a little bit of pig fat every now and then may serve as what Maw Maw used to call "a good old-fashioned cleansing."

The late John Denver used to sing "homegrown tomatoes, homegrown tomatoes—what would life be without homegrown tomatoes? Only two things that money can't buy—that's true love and homegrown tomatoes."

I agree. And a fresh, juicy tomato will taste a little sweeter with a bowl full of fried okra. Maw Maw would approve.

She always knew what was best for me.

LONGING FOR A STEEL GUITAR

Southern Spice, *Times-Georgian*, January 10, 2016

———

Harlan Howard gave us the only definition we'll ever need. When he was asked what makes a great country music song, the prolific songwriter simply replied, "Three chords and the truth."

He left this world in 2002, but when Patsy Cline sang his words "I fall to pieces," I truly believe she did.

Although country music continues to play three chords to most songs, I long for it to return to the truth.

"All things change; some for the good and some for the not so good," said radio disc jockey Red Jones, who is a member of the Georgia Radio Hall of Fame. "Country music has changed, and we're losing the Willie Nelsons of the world. Sadly enough, no one of their caliber is taking their place."

It's hard to believe Keith Urban when he sings "I wish I could take a cab down to the creek and hang a disco ball from an old oak tree."

However, when Loretta tells Conway "You're the reason our kids are ugly," I can picture her actually saying it.

I'm not sure where the demise of country music began, but it likely started around the time Billy Ray Cyrus crooned "Achy Breaky Heart." Cyrus wore white high-top tennis shoes.

Furthermore, I wonder what Porter Wagoner, who probably slept in a pajama jumpsuit adorned with rhinestones, thought of such nonsense?

Even the names of today's country music stars reflect the decline of this genre. Last week's Billboard Top 25 country songs included men's names such as Thomas, Sam, Luke, Jason, Tim, Chris, and Randy.

Where were names like Waylon, Willie, Slim, Hank, Earnest, Jim Ed, Lefty, Leroy, Pee Wee, Floyd, and Merle?

Carrie, Kelsea, and Jana also held spots in the top 25, but I couldn't find a Loretta, Dolly, or Emmylou anywhere in the mix.

Once upon a time, one could turn the radio dial to any country station and recognize the unique voices. Nobody sounds like Nelson, George Jones, or Merle Haggard. These days I can't tell the difference from one song to the next.

Today's country stars all sound alike.

As the world continues to evolve, I'm afraid country music is stuck in the mud with the wrong set of tires. Currently, the number one song in the nation is Thomas Rhett's "Die a Happy Man."

"Between the bottle of wine and the look in your eyes and the Marvin Gaye," sings Rhett. "We danced in the dark under September stars in the pourin' rain."

That ain't country.

Maybe somewhere again in my lifetime, we'll return to real country lyrics such as:

* "I sold a car to a guy who stole my girl, but it don't run, so we're even."
* "Mama get a hammer. There's a fly on Daddy's head."
* "Her teeth were stained, but her heart was pure."
* "She's acting single, and I'm drinkin' doubles."
* "I'm so miserable without you, it's like having you here."
* "I've got Ethyl in my gas tank, but no gal in my arms."
* "I don't know whether to kill myself or go bowling."

Recently, I've found a glimmer of hope in country music. Chris Stapleton looks like somebody who could fix my lawnmower, and I really like the music of a guy whose first name is Sturgill.

As for the rest of the music coming out of Nashville, all I can say is:

"My head hurts. My feet stink. And I don't love you."

WRAPPED WITH LOVE

Southern Spice, *Times-Georgian*, October 4, 2015

———

Every once in a while, what lies behind the sparkling cover beckons me to take a peek.

Sometimes it's a surprise. But it's rarely a disappointment. In some ways unwrapping a gift on my birthday or Christmas still brings me a little joy, but I've reached the age where I'd rather rip into a plate covered with aluminum foil.

Pretty paper with ribbons and bows always signals a celebration. But a plate wrapped in Reynolds Wrap brings peace.

Maybe it takes me back to a time of innocence.

My grandmother Thelma used this magical wrap she called "tinfoil." On Saturday mornings I could count on two things when I spent the night—cartoons and hot biscuits.

While I watched Bugs Bunny and Fred Flintstone, I heard the sounds of pots and pans clinging. And within a few minutes, the smell of bacon and country sausage frying in a black iron skillet filled my senses.

"Oh Joe, my dear, breakfast is ready," she would shout from the kitchen. "Eat what you can, dear. And if you want more later, you can take it home with you."

After breakfast, I would fill the next few hours climbing a tree, throwing a ball in the air or perhaps even tying a bath towel on my back to transform into Batman or Robin. Eventually, my dad would arrive to bring me back home.

After a round of good-byes, I always left with a mountain of food wrapped in tin foil.

Reynolds Wrap was well represented on both sides of my family. My mom's mother, aka Maw Maw, always covered her food with foil. She grew up in hard times and understood the value of a dollar, well almost. When it came to wrapping a piece of pound cake in foil she would use ten yards for just one piece.

"It makes it stay fresh," she often said. "That way if you want to eat it later, it'll still taste good."

The apple didn't far from the tree. My mother inherited Maw Maw's love of keeping everything fresh. She taught us the art of making sure food was always covered up appropriately.

I've clearly been blessed to be surrounded by good women along the way who know the value of love—and, of course—tin foil.

Last night, as I turned off the kitchen lights—I noticed two plates on the counter covered in foil.

I decided to take a peek.

One was cornbread we ate with our vegetable soup, and the other plate contained homemade, chocolate-iced brownies my wife double wrapped.

Some people find peace and serenity when they see a beautiful sunset, the glorious colors of changing leaves in autumn, and a blooming rose. As for me, ripping off a sheet of Reynolds Wrap brings a sense of calm.

When I began my freshman year at the University of Georgia, my mother always handed me a bag of goodies wrapped in foil as I walked out the door.

"You've got sugar cookies, rice crispy treats, a piece of cake, and biscuits left over from this morning," she said. "Make sure you keep it all covered up."

"I can't wait to eat all of this," I said. "I appreciate you doing this, but you don't have to send all of this food every time I leave."

"I know I don't," she replied. "But I want to. I wrapped it with love."

She always did.

FIREFLIES AND A RADIO

Southern Spice, *Times-Georgian*, April 1, 2012

———

He listened to the radio.

On warm summer evenings, as the lightning bugs began their nightly show, my grandfather sat on his porch and rocked in his wicker chair with a radio by his side.

Along with the singing of the crickets as the moon slowly appeared in the sky, announcer Ernie Johnson's voice painted a picture of each swing and pitch, as my grandfather and I listened to a Braves game.

I love baseball.

I love the sound of a wooden bat hitting a ball. I love it's a game of failing often and getting back up again. I love the object of the game is to come home.

Watching a baseball game is still the national pastime, but listening to a game stirs the soul.

Last summer I reconnected with my grandfather's passion for listening to a game. As parents of four boys, my wife and I usually wash dishes, pick up toys, and take out the trash while the Braves play. Thanks to headphones and an iPhone Major League Baseball app, I rediscovered radio and listened to the entire season while we knocked out our nightly chores.

I've been a Braves fan my entire life.

When I was a child, my dad would take my brothers and me to several games every summer. This was a time when the Braves were horrible.

Sometimes, I think we were the only fans in the stadium besides the team's mascot Chief Noc-a-Homa.

When the Braves won their division in 1991, I shouted with joy. I was there when Sid Bream hobbled home to score the winning run in 1992 that propelled the Braves to another World Series.

It was and probably will always be the pinnacle of any game I ever saw or will ever see in person. The crowd was absolutely electric, and the guy who sat in front of me had one of those miniature televisions. When the umpire called Sid safe, that guy's television shattered in a million pieces as he leaped into the air and forgot about it sitting in his lap.

He didn't really seem to care.

"Braves win! Braves win! Braves win!" announced Skip Carey in probably the greatest play-by-play call in the franchise history.

In 2006 while washing my hands in the Delta Crown Room's men's facility in Orlando, I looked to my right and Braves manager Bobby Cox was standing next to me. We struck up a baseball conversation and walked together from the Crown Room to our terminal to board a flight back to Atlanta.

"It's absolutely killing me that we didn't make the playoffs this year," he said.

It was the first time in fourteen seasons the Braves failed to make it to the postseason.

"I promise you one thing," Cox added. "We'll be back there again."

He kept his promise. In his final year as a manager in 2010, the Braves returned to the postseason.

As we reached our terminal, Braves General Manager John Schuerholz and Assistant General Manager Frank Wren waited on Bobby to board the flight. When we arrived back in Atlanta, we shook hands again, and I showed him the cover of my *Sports Illustrated* magazine I read on the airplane.

An artist had painted a picture of the greatest baseball players and managers of all-time for the cover. One person was missing.

"The artist did a great job except one thing," I said to Cox. "Your picture isn't on the cover."

"I don't think it belongs," he replied in his typical modest style. "Let me see that again."

"You can have it," I replied as I gave him my *Sports Illustrated*.

It was the least I could do.

Baseball season is back again. The summer fireflies and crickets will soon return.

I've got my radio ready. Hopefully someday, my dad will give me Granddaddy's chair to go with it.

In the meantime, it's his turn to rock and listen.

Joe (middle) with neighborhood best friends Sam Haney (left) and Joe Murrah (right) at Atlanta-Fulton County Stadium 1978.

LET'S GO RACING

Southern Spice, *Times-Georgian*, February 22, 2015

———

For the boys and girls in the infield, the wall reminds them life's divided in two parts.

"There's a before and after to everything," said local racing expert Matt Carter. "I used to think it was when NASCAR implemented restrictor plate racing. But all that changed when I ran into an old high school classmate."

In 1988, NASCAR changed its rules to level the field when it forced racing teams to install restrictor plates in stock cars, slowing the speed. No longer will we see drivers matching the speed record set by the newest inductee to the Georgia Sports Hall of Fame.

"Awesome Bill from Dawsonville, the great Bill Elliot will more than likely hold the record forever that he set in Talladega in 1987 at 212 miles per hour," said Carter. "It's been almost thirty years since the rules changed and fans still complain."

"So is that the before and after for stock car fans?" I asked.

"Oh no, my high school buddy made it clear when I ran into him that day," said Carter. "I said to him 'Man, I haven't seen you in a long time. How's everything going in your life?'"

"He looked at me with sad eyes and shook his head," continued Carter. "As he combed his fingers through his hair, he said, 'Not good. Things ain't been the same since Dale died.'"

For many NASCAR fans, the day Dale Earnhardt died after hitting the wall on the final lap of the 2001 Daytona 500 marks the before and after in the world of racing. Once again, the engines will be roaring as the "Great American Race" gets underway this afternoon. And once again, fans will pause to reflect on the life of Earnhardt, who was often referred to as the "Intimidator."

NASCAR has definitely missed the man who drove the black Number 3 Chevrolet. There's been nobody like him since.

"You go back to the start of time," Earnhardt once said. "One cave guy was fighting another cave guy because his club was bigger than his or his woman had longer hair. That's competition."

For a few years, I watched Earnhardt navigate the racetrack at the Talladega Superspeedway. The majority of the crowd held up three fingers in his honor each time he passed.

But perhaps no one honored Earnhardt more than a woman I saw in the Talladega infield on a scorching, hot Alabama Sunday afternoon. I heard a roar before the race began from a group of young men. When I turned to see the commotion, a girl was sitting atop a Trans Am waving to the crowd. And then, in NASCAR style, she lifted her shirt and exposed herself to the crowd.

I looked.

As Mark Twain once said, "There is a great deal of human nature in people."

And then, I looked again. It wasn't her bare chest that caught my eye as much as Earnhardt's trademark "#3" tattooed on her left bosom.

She eventually covered herself as the young men continued to whistle. It was the first and last time I ever saw a Dale Earnhardt tattoo in such a place.

My guess is the girl never showed her daddy the "#3" body mark. Then again, if you've ever been to Talladega, I wouldn't be surprised. But who am I to judge?

That's what I love about NASCAR. People from all walks of life—young and old, black and white, rich and poor, tall and short, skinny and a lot of fat people—coming together to watch cars go around a race track. Even though I've yet to put a tattoo on my body, I share a connection to the young girl who lifted her shirt.

I'm sure like Matt Carter's friend and me, this girl would agree: "Things ain't been the same since Dale died."

A HAIRY AWAKENING

Southern Spice, *Times-Georgian*, March 10, 2013

———

My first chest hair appeared when I was thirteen. It felt like it would never arrive. I had no idea at the time this was part of growing up. I thought chest hair grew because I followed the orders of the older kids in my neighborhood.

Before turning into a teenager, the older kids in my neighborhood would make my friends and me do things we despised. They made us eat hot red peppers, wrestle each other until someone had blood running from his nose, and so many other things.

Why did we allow this?

We wanted to join their neighborhood club. We wanted to be like them. And we were ignorant enough to do everything they asked.

There was really no reason to tolerate their torture, but we did. We could have easily run home and told our parents, but the older kids had a way of motivating us with the following magic words—"Do what we ask you to do, don't tell mom or dad, and it will put hair on your chest."

That was it.

My friends and I decided all of the older kid hazing in the world was clearly worth it for the reassurance and promise it would one day put hair on our chests.

It was the 1970s and chest hair was all the rage. Whether it was Burt Reynolds sporting a hairy chest in *Smokey and the Bandit* or any man willing to shed his tie, open his collar, and don a dapper leisure suit, every boy in my neighborhood wanted only two things in life—1) a poster of Farrah Fawcett and 2) chest hair.

For the majority of my life, I've admired men sprouting hairy chests. My generation always honored these men in the same way previous generations respected John Wayne. Only recently, while sitting on a beach in Ft. Lauderdale, did I receive the ultimate awakening.

"It's time to consider shedding your chest hair," said my millennial generation sister-in-law Lucie Anne.

"Are you saying other people sitting around us aren't finding me attractive," I replied. "If I decide to shave, don't you think it will make my belly look larger?"

"You're still stuck in the '70s," she said.

I think she's right. I still long to watch *The Love Boat* and *Fantasy Island* on Saturday nights and still dream of taking a trip to Texarkana in a black Trans Am, with a Jerry Reed song playing on the car radio.

This new epiphany of realizing chest hair is no longer considered stylish and cool among the younger generation has leveled me into reality.

I've truly reached middle age. Besides, my chest hair has already started turning gray.

Even the people who I bicycle with have started shaving their legs, because it's what the professionals in the Tour de France do. We've come to learn these professional cyclists also supplement their bodies with steroids and lord knows what else.

I'm keeping my leg hair.

A few years ago, I had the opportunity to attend a lecture in Phoenix, Arizona, by Frank Abagnale, Jr., who achieved worldwide fame in Steven Spielberg's movie *Catch Me if You Can*, starring Leonardo DiCaprio. He told the real story behind the movie, and how his wife and the FBI character portrayed by Tom Hanks in the movie helped him turn his life into something positive.

"A real man loves his family," said Abagnale, Jr. "A real man spends time with his family."

24

He's right. A real man is someone who loves others. A real man strives to be all he can possibly be.

And even though my sister-in-law disagrees, I still argue a real man has a hairy chest.

HENNY PENNY

Southern Spice, *Times-Georgian*, September 7, 2014

———

Cluck, cluck.

And a cock-a-doodle, doodle-doo. It looks like one flew over the chicken coop.

As the rest of the world argues political conflicts and an outbreak of war, Carroll County has its own issues. Let's call it "ChickenGate."

Recently, the Carroll County Board of Commissioners held a public meeting to discuss the proposed ordinance that would allow up to eight hens and no roosters on a residential zoned lot of 1.5 acres or less.

For lots greater than 1.5 acres, 12 hens would be permitted and no roosters, as long as they were kept 25 feet from the property lines. The county already allows chickens and other livestock on lots of four acres or more that are zoned agricultural.

As the farm-to-table movement continues to sweep our region so has the interest in backyard poultry. Hens are laying eggs from Sunset Hills to Cross Plains.

"I ate an egg this morning," said local resident Dr. Tee Reeve. "There's nothing like going to my neighbor's yard and grabbing a couple to scramble."

Based on the numbers in attendance at last week's meeting, it's safe to say Carroll County has a passion for poultry.

In order to understand this new trend, I traveled to a farm outside of Tyus to interview the world-famous Henny Penny, aka Chicken Little.

"I've never really understood what's the difference in having twelve hens versus thirteen," said Chicken Little. "Of course, there's a lot of truth in the old saying about having 'Too many hens in the hen house.' Hens are very competitive."

"What about the roosters?" I asked. "They almost got shut out."

"Oh, we never liked them anyway," replied Chicken Little. "Roosters can't understand why we hens need peace and quiet in the morning (cluck, cluck). Or why it's best they don't speak to us until after 11:00 a.m. After all these years, they don't get it. They want to wake us up as the sun's rising not realizing we need at least another hour or two of beauty sleep."

"Last Tuesday, the board voted unanimously to take the ordinance off the table and communicated it will likely pass no chicken ordinance anytime soon," I said. "It's a big win for poultry. How do you feel about the board's decision?"

"Since I live in somebody's backyard, it doesn't matter," replied Chicken Little. "It's a lot worse for some of my cousins who live on big farms. They all know when the Pilgrim's Pride truck shows up it's not going to be a good day (cluck, cluck). So when we see a chicken truck pass by our house, we say a little prayer and hope they'll have a good resting spot, like KFC, Big Chic, or the Monday special at Billy Bob's BBQ."

I thanked my hen friend Chicken Little for expanding my perspective and asked her one more question as I left.

"Is it true the chicken came before the egg?" I asked.

"You better believe we did (cluck, cluck)," Chicken Little replied. "Trust me. My great grandfather Rooster Cogburn told me so and he was always right."

And I believe my friend. Besides, she's the one who told us the sky was falling.

WALKING IN MEMPHIS

Southern Spice, *Times-Georgian*, August 18, 2013

———

I boarded the plane without my blue suede shoes.

Even my sideburns were missing, along with a leather jacket. Instead, I packed a swimsuit along with a Patagonia fleece windbreaker because I didn't know where we were going.

"Why don't we get a group of guys together and drive to the airport tonight?" said my friend Tee Green. "Let's set a budget and go to the ticket counter and take the cheapest flight to wherever and fly back on Sunday. If it's over $200, we'll drive back to Carrollton."

Without hesitation, I agreed to this adventure, along with my friends Mike Duncan and Jim Watters. We were all in our twenties, single, no children, and the only commitment we had was to return to our jobs on Monday morning.

When I informed my mother of our trip, she quickly responded— "I'll be glad when all of you boys get over Fool's Hill."

"Be safe," she said. "And please let someone know where y'all are staying in case something happens. I'll pray y'all there and back."

After a few minutes at the AirTran counter, we had a choice to fly roundtrip to either Memphis or Tampa. Since half of the group wanted seafood and the other half craved barbecue, we settled it the old fashioned way—we flipped a coin.

Memphis won the toss, and within an hour we boarded the plane destined for dry-rubbed ribs and the home of the King.

Once we arrived in downtown Memphis, we stopped at a hotel to find a place to stay only to realize the Promise Keepers Convention was in town, and there was no vacancy anywhere. Since Memphis was booked we drove to the outskirts of the city in search of an inn. Luckily, we found a room at a Tunica, Mississippi casino.

That was about the only luck we had at the casino.

We filled the next two days listening to the blues at B. B. King's club on Beale Street and eating dry-rubbed ribs at the world famous Rendezvous. And, of course, we toured the home of the King.

This week marks thirty-six years since I heard the news of Elvis's death, while watching an episode of *Emergency* on Channel 11. Hardly a day goes by when I don't have an Elvis song playing in my head. As for Graceland, I've toured it twice and can easily check it off my bucket list. However, I could visit the Jungle Room once again, if persuaded.

Thankfully, we all survived the trip and reported to our jobs on time Monday morning. I'm glad none of us had to weigh in because I came back ten pounds heavier from too much barbecue.

By nature, I tend to plan trips ahead of time. If I'm going to Chicago, I'll research days in advance where to find the best hot dog. If I'm traveling to Dallas or Fort Worth, I'll research where to find the best brisket. Even if I plan to take a journey down Bankhead Avenue in Carrollton, Georgia, I'll research the best hamburger and onion rings on that side of town (it's Millie's Pub & Eatery).

Sometimes, however, it's the spur-of-the-moment trip that's the most fun. To hop in a car, train, or airplane and move with the wind ignites a spark in our lives.

There's no doubt these types of journeys create memorable moments. Life is full of surprises each day. Some of those we can't control like the wind or the rain. Other surprises, however, we have the ability to create.

Luckily, I've had many of these experiences. Life is too short and complex. I plan to mix more of these spur-of-the moment adventures into the time I have left. Life's still teaching me.

It's amazing what one learns while climbing Fool's Hill.

CATCHER KNOWS BEST

Southern Spice, *Times-Georgian,* June 1, 2014

———

There were no strikes.

For the first six batters, I couldn't hit Jeff Turner's catcher's mitt. The umpire almost fell asleep, as his job became easy, since all he had to shout was "ball four."

At the age of eight years old, I made my pitching debut for the Haney's Drug Corner team, and we were battling Southwire for first place in the Carrollton Parks and Recreation Department's Mite League.

"Just throw a strike," I heard Jeff's mother, Stephanie, shout from the stands.

That's when Jeff called timeout and approached the mound for my first pitcher-catcher conference.

"You sure you don't want to move back to playing second base?" Jeff asked.

I shook my head and stared at the next hitter.

It wasn't just anyone stepping to the plate. It was Joe Murrah. He was my best friend, Chapel Heights neighbor, and member of our neighborhood secret society we called "The Moes" (named after legendary pitcher Moe Drabowsky).

And he walked to the batter's box with a smile.

For a moment, I knew this wasn't only about Haney's Drug Corner versus Southwire. Since Joe's next door neighbor was Tommy Haney, who sponsored my team, it was about something bigger.

It was about neighborhood pride.

As Jeff Turner crouched in his catcher's position, he gave me the only sign we had—to throw a pitch over the plate.

The first pitch was low and away. The second wasn't much better as I threw one high and inside to let Joe know I wasn't going to back down. Finally, the third pitch was like a musical symphony singing from the sky above Lake Carroll when the umpire shouted, "Steeeeriiiike one!"

It would take only two more pitches.

I threw the next one right over the plate, and Joe foul tipped it up the first base line. And then the stare-down occurred. I shook my head, as if Jeff really was giving me a signal, and moved into the windup.

Joe took a step forward and then took a swing and barely missed as the umpire screamed, "Hallelujah, pitcher, strike three, batter—you're out."

I threw my arms into the air as if I had won Game Seven of the World Series and then returned to my old ways. I walked the next three batters and the umpire called the inning due to the tenth-batter rule.

When we returned to the dugout, Jeff looked me in the eyes and said, "It's probably best you don't throw your arms into the air and celebrate when you just walked nine batters. Think about going back to playing second base."

Jeff, Joe, and I would go on to play on various ball teams together through the next several years. We even played together for the Carrollton Trojans in high school where Jeff had a stellar career that led to signing with Shorter College, and Joe won the Most Valuable Player award our senior year.

As for me, I ended my career with a .172 batting average.

For the last few months, I followed Jeff's two sons Andrew and Sam, who played a crucial role for the Carrollton Trojans baseball team's path to the Georgia state championship.

They played with incredible motivation, drive, and heart.

Andrew, convincingly, made the greatest nab in the school's history when he robbed a homerun against LaGrange. (Type in the search words

"Andrew Turner Spectacular Catch" on YouTube to view.) Fittingly, he collected the final out of the season to clinch the state title on another remarkable grab.

Congratulations to the Trojans on such an outstanding baseball season. The team will forever be argued as the school's best ever.

And I will forever refer to Andrew's play as "The Catch."

As for Andrew's dad's comments I should return to second base after walking nine batters and celebrating Joe Murrah's strikeout, I now refer to his words as "Good Advice."

LANCE'S TIGHT LEGACY

Southern Spice, *Times-Georgian*, September 9, 2012

———

I t wasn't a good summer for the Armstrong family.

After defying the odds of even returning to pedal a bicycle, Lance Armstrong won the Tour de France seven times after a bout with testicular cancer.

I don't know about you, but to me the words "testicular cancer" and "bicycle seat" go together about as well as Clint Eastwood at a Democratic Party fundraiser.

The recent news of the USAA's decision to strip Armstrong of his seven titles and to ban him from competitive cycling was a blow to so many fans, but it's his return from cancer that still stands out—or so I thought.

"Doped or clean, winning seven straight Tour de France competitions is impressive, but that pales in comparison to Lance Armstrong's greatest accomplishment," said local cycling expert Matt Carter, who pedaled a Huffy as a youngster. "This guy single handedly made it OK for millions of men to believe it acceptable to wear tight bicycle shorts."

That's true.

Look at the growing number of cyclists leaving the parking lot of Perpetual Motion Bicycles in Carrollton on Tuesday nights. Although the number of men cycling and wearing tight bike shorts may be growing,

I hope this trend doesn't spark a new line of men's hunting and fishing attire or make the cover of *L. L. Bean.*

"It's not only cycling," observed Carter. "Walk through a men's department store and you'll find tight shirts, skinny jeans, and too close for comfort underwear."

Who actually gets to wear this type of clothing and look good after the age of sixteen? What do these men in skinny jeans eat?

Obviously, I don't run in the same circles with the tight shirt crowd. For some reason, these skinny jean guys never seem to stand in line with me at the local critically acclaimed fried poultry establishment Big Chic.

Last year, when I returned to my childhood hobby of bicycling, I walked into Perpetual Motion only to hear those dreaded words from owner Allen Griffin.

"You're going to want to wear tight bike clothing like Lance Armstrong if you're going to cycle several miles per week on your road bike," Griffin told me.

"Besides, if you don't think women find cyclists sexy, then you need to go to a professional race to see for yourself."

My wife is obviously not one of these women when she sees me walk out the door wearing tight pants.

That's why I choose to ride in black cycling clothes while the rooster is literally crowing. Johnny Cash wore black for "the poor and beaten down." I wear black for the men who have the "done lop" syndrome.

That's when your belly has "done lopped" over your belt buckle.

Even football jerseys have gone the tight route. Watch an old college football game on ESPN Classic, and the jerseys were bigger than the players in the 1970s and 1980s. The only sport to buck this trend has been basketball, as their shorts and jerseys have grown longer compared to the tight-skinned uniforms of the 1950s.

Unfortunately, Lance no longer holds his titles and his career statistics will have asterisks next to his records, but his comeback from cancer and his LIVESTRONG Foundation continue to inspire and empower cancer survivors throughout the world.

Maybe local cycling expert and former Huffy owner Matt Carter is right. Maybe we can give Lance credit for making it cool to wear tight shorts while cycling as an adult.

Maybe it's just…part of the package.

Local expert Matt Carter (Batman) and Joe (Robin) donning masks, capes and tight pants as the Caped Crusaders for the 1974 Pack 138 Cub Scouts parade.

TRADING MEMORIES

Southern Spice, *Times-Georgian,* June 24, 2012

―――

e used to walk through the woods with a briefcase.

In the early 1980s, my Central Middle School classmate David Sheinin would dodge the briars and pinecones as he walked through the woods that separated his house on Edgewood Drive from my quarters in Chapel Heights.

He didn't come to play. He came to trade.

David and I began our friendship trading baseball cards. He built an incredible collection from scratch. I built my collection the old-fashioned way—I inherited it from my older brothers.

We would make trades. Some were good. Some were not so good, but we each built a heck of a collection.

Although we didn't realize it at the time, these skills would one day be the early training ground for our future careers.

Recently, a story aired on *CBS Sunday Morning* titled "Collectors of Baseball Cards Striking Out." According to the report, "Over the years, the art of collecting baseball cards has changed drastically, from a child-hood hobby to a billion-dollar industry. Today the market for those collectibles is rapidly collapsing."

"It's too bad that the industry got so cutthroat and corporate that it sucked the joy out of it as a hobby and eventually led to the demise of the whole industry," said Central Lion Hall of Famer and award-winning journalist David Sheinin, who is now the national baseball writer for *The*

Washington Post. "I remember one stepping-stone on the way to oblivion: the year they stopped putting that awful-tasting, pasty bubblegum in the new packs of cards because the gum could leave a mark and lessen the value of whatever card it was touching."

My mother probably drove 12,000 miles in her wood panel station wagon hauling my brothers and friends around Carrollton to find a convenience store that sold baseball cards. They were a hot commodity in the 1970s as stores would sell out sometimes the same day the new packages of cards arrived.

My goal every year was to collect every card. We didn't collect cards as an investment. (We never knew baseball cards would become a billion dollar plus industry.)

We collected cards so we could play each other in a dice game.

"If you rolled two sixes, it was a homerun," said Carrollton native and Emmy Award winner Mark Parkman, who will spend the summer in London as the operations executive for Olympic Broadcasting Services. "I still have all my baseball cards and even my notebook I used to keep statistics on each player. My mother will be happy to know I kept them, because she's still waiting on her cut of the profits should I ever sell them."

In the 1980s, the baseball card industry exploded as all of the sudden investors viewed the cards as valuable. Card conventions and trade shows started showing up every weekend in the big cities.

When I realized our Pete Rose rookie card was worth enough to provide a free college education for my brothers and me, I quickly searched and found the card only to discover someone had crossed out "outfield" as his position and with an ink-pen wrote "second base" on the card.

It's still worthless.

"I used to make my parents drive me around to card shows all over the state and at one of these shows, I traded a well-preserved Pete Rose rookie card for a 1933 Babe Ruth card that had giant creases down the middle and frayed corners," said Sheinin. "Even though it was a terrible trade for me, in terms of value, I simply wanted a Babe Ruth card. I mean, how cool was that—to own a fifty-year-old baseball card of the Sultan of Swat? I still have that Babe Ruth card."

My brothers and I still have all of our baseball cards although I haven't looked at them in years. Times have changed and anyone can search for a baseball player's photo and statistics in a matter of seconds via the internet.

It's almost as if the demise of baseball cards reflects much more than a dying industry. It's the passing of the torch from a slower paced world of card collecting to a world of rapid, high speed information and overload.

Today iPads are replacing briefcases.

"Oh, and that 'briefcase' you recall was actually a handmade wooden box, with dividing slats perfectly calibrated for baseball cards, constructed by my stepfather, Bill Lowry," Sheinin added. "I still have it—right under the desk where I work right now—and it's still full of baseball cards."

David Sheinin doesn't walk through the woods anymore to talk baseball. He now leaves his office at *The Washington Post* and walks into every major league ballpark and press box in the country.

I'm glad his passion for baseball still shines, but most importantly— I'm glad he kept the briefcase.

DROOL SCHOOL

Southern Spice, *Times-Georgian*, August 2, 2015

———

N obody spits anymore.

Oh sure, you'll see an athlete or a runner occasionally let saliva fly in the brutal humidity of a Georgia summer. And there's the baseball player who will let a few salty sunflower seeds leap from his mouth.

But nobody spits for the sake of spitting.

I learned to spit by watching my great-aunt Lizzie drool in a Maxwell House coffee can after a Sunday lunch on Maw Maw's front porch. My cousins and I were a little scared of her and her snuff.

We thought she possessed supernatural powers.

"I dare you to go hide Aunt Lizzie's snuff," my cousin Bill once tempted me.

"No way," I replied. "Aunt Lizzie will put a spell on me."

As I grew older, I observed my brother Bob and his friends Johnny and Tim perfect the art of spitting.

My buddies and I would often spy on them through the bushes outside the Carrollton First United Methodist Church after a Sunday evening service. We weren't close enough to hear what they were talking about, but we were amazed at how far they could spit.

It's funny how you're impressed with such things when you're eight years old.

One day I tried to mimic them when the older boys noticed me struggling.

"You need to learn how to hawk a loogy like a man and hit a rock," Johnny lectured me.

Within a few minutes, Johnny taught me how to fill my lungs with air, allow the saliva to flow on my tongue, and release it in the air at just the right time. After five minutes, I felt as if I had joined an elite fraternity and was a member of the spitters' brotherhood.

Those days are long gone and so are the men who didn't care what others thought about their disgusting habits. If they felt like spitting, they did. And it never failed one of the most common places to watch these men in action was on Sunday mornings.

"I miss those men who would shake the preacher's hand walking out of church, take a couple of steps, spit, and then proceed to light up a Marlboro," said local etiquette expert Matt Carter. "Men are too busy with technology these days. They'd rather check their iPhones than spittle some saliva and light a Winston cigarette after worship service."

Maybe it's best spitting is a dying art.

I'm sure all of our mommas would be proud of the way the times are changing and boys are minding their manners. But I must confess I'm confused by my generation.

Men today can't sit still. They're too busy taking boot camp classes, shooting sporting targets, and training to run marathons.

Nobody wants to slow down and play checkers anymore. Nobody wants to rock in a front porch swing for hours at a time. And nobody wants to sit around a wood fire stove, telling lies, and spitting.

And that's the sputtering truth.

COAST TO COAST

Southern Spice, *Times-Georgian*, June 22, 2014

———

A long distance dedication became a ritual.

I didn't have to travel far. Only a few feet away from my bed, an old radio brought me the weekly story of some person separated from a loved one.

These were the days before cell phones, text messaging, and Xboxes. Long distance telephone calls became a luxury and only permitted under extreme circumstances.

If rain fell on Saturday mornings, a young boy either drove his parents crazy or he found something to do. Usually it involved a little of both, but eventually I would grab my Batman and Robin action figures and create a make-believe Gotham City in my bedroom. For a few hours, the dynamic duo would defeat the Joker, Penguin, and Riddler.

But I was never alone.

Always in the background, a voice located in Southern California traveled the airwaves via Carrollton radio station WPPI to bring me the weekly sounds of the current top forty songs in America.

Casey Kasem was always with me.

Last week, Kasem died at the age of 82. For four decades, Kasem counted down the country's most popular songs on his weekly show *American Top 40*. Although I quit listening to the show years ago, Casey was as much a part of my childhood as the Easter Bunny, Santa Claus, and Tooth Fairy, only he brought me something every week.

He brought me music. And that's one of the greatest gifts of all.

"Music is a moral law," wrote the great philosopher Plato. "It gives soul to the universe, wings to the mind, flight to the imagination, and charm and gaiety to life and to everything."

I continue to surround myself with music throughout each day. In some way, however, it's gotten too easy.

There's a tiny iPod that holds thousands of songs I've accumulated through the years. There's satellite radio with hundreds of genres to suit any musical taste.

In other words, it's like having my hand on the thermostat at all times as I can pick and choose what I want to listen to each day.

It hasn't always been like that.

Whether I liked or disliked the songs on Casey's weekly countdown, I didn't have much of a choice. Usually, I was stuck with Casey.

"When we are no longer able to change a situation, we are challenged to change ourselves," wrote the late Austrian neurologist and Holocaust survivor, Victor Frankl, in his book *Man's Search for Meaning.* "Everything can be taken from a man, but one thing: the last of the human freedoms—to choose one's attitude in any given set of circumstances, to choose one's own way."

Being stuck inside your room on a rainy Saturday morning isn't so bad. It's nowhere even close to those who've suffered concentration camps or any institution that robs your freedom.

For a child, however, his mind doesn't comprehend that true happiness is derived from the "inside/out," not the "outside/in."

There's a wonderful scene from the movie *The Shawshank Redemption* when the main character Andy Dufresne is locked up for two weeks in isolation. When he returns, his friends ask him how he survived.

"It was the easiest time I ever did," replied Andy. "I had Mr. Mozart to keep me company (as he points and taps his head). It was in here (as he gestures over his heart). That's the beauty of music. They can't get that from you."

And no one can ever take away the music stored inside of me—or you. Even as I watch my mother lose most of her verbal communication skills due to Alzheimer's, she still can hear the music.

So Casey, if you're listening, please send my mom and all of those struggling a song and a long distance dedication today. And, oh yeah, don't forget to tell them to "keep your feet on the ground, and keep reaching for the stars."

Until next week, "we'll see you on the radio."

THIRTY STRAIGHT AT THE GULF

Southern Spice, *Times-Georgian*, April 8, 2012

———

Seagrove Beach, Florida—I like to relax on spring break. As my family and I are enjoying a short trip to the Gulf Coast, I'm finally catching up on some needed rest.

I also like to eat on spring break.

One morning when I left my wife's grandfather's condominium parking lot to Highway 30-A, it seemed like hundreds of spring breakers were already awake and outside walking, running, or riding a bike, as I passed through Alys Beach and Rosemary Beach.

Where was I going?

I was going to get doughnuts, or as they spell it on the Gulf Coast—"donuts."

I've been making the journey to Thomas Donut & Snack Shop on the western edge of Panama City Beach since I was twelve years old. Founded in 1971, the shop has lines that are usually half of a football field long, but well worth the wait to bite into a chocolate glazed, blueberry, or red velvet doughnut. I learned the secret many years ago to go inside to order as the lines are usually shorter than the outside windows which are filled with first-timers.

"You must be from around here?" a man asked me while I stood in line inside the building. "Only the locals know the secret."

"Let's just say I've been here a time or two in my life," I responded as it hit me that this is my thirtieth consecutive year of eating at Thomas's.

When I returned to the condo, my wife looked at my two bags of doughnuts and suddenly began to quiz me like a trial attorney.

"Two dozen doughnuts?" she asked. "You talk all the time how you need to eat healthier, and you return with two dozen doughnuts. How many doughnuts do you think we actually will eat?"

I didn't even bother to argue my case. She clearly won. I decided to eat another doughnut.

Although my quest for doughnuts in the morning satisfies my sugar craving, I'm spending the rest of my time hanging out with my family, reading a good book, and observing the thousands of dazed and confused teenagers who walk around with their heads bowed. No, they aren't praying. They are texting and checking their cell phones for important information.

My wife and I co-teach a teenage Sunday school class at St. Margaret's Church with longtime Carroll County physician Jim Rash. A few months ago when our discussion moved to technology, he told our students that he refers to their generation as the "Bent-Neck Generation."

"You all are the first generation who spend more time looking at your cell phones than you do your friends," he told them. "Your necks are always bent instead of looking your friends in the eye."

His observation generated laughter among the group including myself because we all realize how we easily can become addicted to cell phones and how time spent with "bent necks" can have negative consequences to our friends, family, and others.

These teenagers on spring break need to take a break from their cell phones, spend more time appreciating the breathtaking beauty of the Gulf of Mexico and eat a doughnut.

Yesterday, I again watched the swarms of beach exercisers and felt a sense of guilt come over me because I was not among them. But then as I returned to the condo to unload another round of doughnuts, I saw an ambulance and two fire trucks across the street tend to a road cyclist who was struck by a car. Thankfully, he was OK.

As he moved back on the road, I felt a sense relief. So I did what I felt was appropriate at that time—I said a small prayer for the cyclist, and then I ate another doughnut.

PART II
AUTUMN

———

Life starts all over again when it gets crisp in the fall.

—F. Scott Fitzgerald, *The Great Gatsby*, 1925

LET MY PEOPLE GO

Southern Spice, *Times-Georgian,* May 22, 2016

———

A s I walked to the sink, an attractive woman started smiling at me.

I smiled back, and then I proceeded to wash my hands. When I reached for the paper towel, another woman walked towards me and also smiled at me.

Once again, I smiled back.

"I actually think two women were hitting on me," I told my wife when I returned to the table where we were dining at the outdoor restaurant Caliza in Alys Beach, Florida, last summer. "That's the first time I've been in a coed bathroom since my trip to Europe a few years ago."

"The bathrooms here aren't coed," she gasped. "Oh my gosh, you just used the women's bathroom."

"Well that explains why there were no stand up urinals," I laughed.

"I can't believe you used the women's bathroom," she said as she almost fell out of her seat laughing at me.

I haven't been in a women's bathroom since.

For the last several weeks, the world has watched the North Carolina legislature's stance on its anti-transgender law and how far it plans to go to defend it. Since I've never really paid attention to who's standing at the stall next to me, I'm hoping we focus on bigger issues such as teaching men how to aim, so I don't have to stand in a puddle of "tee-tee" the next time I'm in the bathroom at Sanford Stadium.

The modern day Archie Bunkers of the world have their underdrawers in a wad over such a trivial issue. It's not like transgender people have recently started using the bathroom in public places. It's been going on for years.

Since I now have experience of spending time in both women's and men's restrooms, I truly see a difference. Men usually don't talk to each other in the bathroom. They don't acknowledge anyone is even there. They get the job done and get out.

Women, obviously, smile at any man who seems to have lost his way and entered their domain.

I don't have the answer to solving this issue so we no longer discriminate against any of our brothers and sisters. But I believe one doesn't have to look any further than Stripling Chapel Road in Carrollton, Georgia.

For years while in operation, the Front Porch Restaurant served some of the county's best fried catfish, chicken, hush puppies, and sweet tea. When its founder and owner, the late Dorsey Duffey, started this fried gastro smorgasbord in the late 1970s, he was years ahead of the times.

Duffey, an avid hunter, loved everything about nature and the great outdoors. When CB radios became the rage, he simply carried the handle "Bird Dog" on the local airwaves. It was only fitting when it was time to put the gender signs on the bathroom doors at the Front Porch, Duffey knew what was best.

Instead of using today's buzzwords of Men and Women, Duffey left the decision up to his customers. He wanted everyone to feel welcome. All they had to do was decide as they looked at the bathroom doors.

The signs simply read Pointers and Setters.

DON'T MESS WITH MAW MAW

Southern Spice, *Times-Georgian*, February 17, 2013

Maw Maw carried a pistol.

This was long before gun control issues dominated the political rhetoric of Congress and the White House. She kept one at hand after Paw Paw died in 1975, since she lived alone. As far as I know, she never fired at anyone, but she once allowed my brother Bob and his friend Johnny Tanner to go outside her house and shoot at a Coca-Cola can.

"We only shot her .44 Magnum pistol once because it knocked me and Bob on our tails when we fired it," said Johnny. "Maw Maw thought it was funny."

I always felt safe when I was around my late grandmother Inice Green of Bowdon, who I called "Maw Maw." One time when I was eight years old, my mother needed to stop by Rich's Department Store in Atlanta to return an item from Christmas. She parked her wood panel station wagon in a parking garage and asked me and Maw Maw to stay in the vehicle while she exchanged her gift.

"You take your time," said Maw Maw. "He's safe with me."

A few minutes later, a group of guys entered the parking garage and began fighting about twenty-five yards from our station wagon.

"Don't you worry," she said to me. "They're not going to bother us."

That's when I noticed Maw Maw reach next to her Social Security card in her purse and pull out something from a brown paper bag.

"Maw Maw, is that your pistol?" I asked peering over the backseat.

"Yes," she replied. "I'm not going to use it unless these boys try to jump in our car."

Thankfully, those boys resolved their issue and moved on. I'm glad because they had no idea my grandmother, who always smiled and was so kind and sweet, carried the same type of pistol in her pocket book that Clint Eastwood used in the *Dirty Harry* movies.

Recently, my family visited New Orleans to spend time with friends and relatives. I've always loved the Big Easy. I've always celebrated their priorities of food, fun, and fellowship.

As my family walked the streets in the French Quarter, my wife admired the architecture while my children enjoyed being in a city they'd never visited. As for me, I thought about Maw Maw pulling out her pistol on Bourbon Street in 1976.

That summer my parents decided to pack us in their station wagon and visit my Uncle Bobby and Aunt Beverly in Houston, Texas. One of our stops along this trip was New Orleans. While my dad drove us through Bourbon Street at night, he needed to make a pit stop.

"You run in, and I'll watch all of them," Maw Maw instructed my dad. When my dad exited the vehicle, Maw Maw reached in her pocket book and pulled out her .44 Magnum from a brown paper bag. "Nobody's going to mess with us."

In the months ahead, Congress and the White House will continue to debate and implement new gun control laws. I try to think what Maw Maw would have thought about all of this? My guess is she could have cared less as long as she could continue to own her pistol.

On the other hand, if the government ever tried to restrict her homemade remedy cough syrup and Vicks salve—that may have sparked another revolution.

Inice "Maw Maw" Green

BREAKING BOUNDARIES

Southern Spice, *Times-Georgian*, September 8, 2013

———

S he didn't succeed at first.

This past week I eagerly awaited the news of endurance swimmer Diana Nyad's bid to conquer the 110-mile passage from Cuba to Florida she first tried 35 years ago. After four failed attempts due to jellyfish stings and dehydration, the 64-year-old swimmer emerged 53 hours later on the surf on Smathers Beach in Key West, Florida.

I'm in awe of those individuals throughout our world history who've broken the boundaries. From Chuck Yeager having the guts to pilot a jet to break the sound barrier to Roger Bannister running a mile under four minutes, it's these boundary breakers who inspire and teach us we can do what was once considered impossible.

I've never had the opportunity to meet those individuals who've changed history and are featured in textbooks across the land. However, that doesn't mean the west Georgia area has never produced any boundary breakers. It has.

"I remember a guy I'll refer to as Landon to protect his identity," said my brother Bob. "One day while sitting in the Carrollton High cafeteria in 1977, a group of my friends watched the construction crews finish installing the new state-of-the-art lights at Grisham Stadium. Just as we talked about how high the new light poles were, Landon spoke up."

"I'm going to climb one of the light poles on Wednesday night at 8:30," Landon told the group with a poker face as his muscles bulged from his Bruce Springsteen concert T-shirt.

"It was almost like that scene in the Paul Newman movie *Cool Hand Luke* when Luke declared he was going to eat fifty eggs," said Bob.

No one doubted Landon, as word quickly spread.

"I think he expected just a small group to show up, but Landon drew a crowd in excess of one hundred classmates," said Bob. "He even had his signature Mohawk hairstyle groomed for the event."

As Landon began his climb, the crowd suddenly scattered like ants.

"That's when Coach Vernon Wilkes arrived, and then the law enforcement showed up," said Bob. "Landon's stunt was over."

"None of us got in trouble because, as the police arrived, we all heard a screeching sound from what is now Ben Scott Boulevard," said Bob. "One of our classmates was drag racing his Chevy Chevelle against a guy from Temple. Just as the police and the students ran to see what was going on, the guy from Temple ran off the road and crashed into Buffalo Swamp. Thankfully everyone was OK. I guess you could say our classmate won the race."

And like Diana Nyad who failed her first few attempts to break a new boundary, Landon refused to quit.

"The next day at school he told our lunch table to not spread the word, and he would attempt to climb again," said Bob. "That night our small group watched Landon climb to the top of the light pole as we cheered from below."

I'm always curious at the words of wisdom these boundary breakers relay to our world following their achievements. Nyad spoke to encourage others.

"I have three messages," she told reporters. "One is we should never, ever give up. Two is you never are too old to chase your dreams. Three is it looks like a solitary sport, but it takes a team."

As local folklore around Landon's famous climb still surfaces, his words probably won't be regarded as eloquent as Nyad's. He chose words that one may argue as more personal when he shouted from the top:

"I'm crazy. I'm crazy."

ELVIS AND ME

Southern Spice, *Times-Georgian,* January 22, 2012

———

E lvis half-raised me.

As a four-year-old child, my mother could tend to other household chores while I would take afternoon naps on the floor in front of her RCA stereo. She would put an Elvis album on the turntable, and I would fall asleep halfway through "Love Me Tender."

Occasionally, she would experiment with albums from John Denver, Eddie Arnold, and Freddy Fender, but it was the King who could soothe me to sleep every time.

I'll never forget the August day in 1977 when I heard Elvis had died. While I watched firefighters Roy Desoto and Johnny Gage extinguish a fire on a repeat episode of *Emergency,* the report scrolled across the television. In total shock, I hopped on my bicycle and rode over to my friend Sam Haney's house, where we gathered around his television to watch the coverage.

I was crushed.

My mother had promised to take me to Elvis's next concert in Atlanta, but the King was gone. He would never live to record the famous song "Margaritaville," which was supposed to headline his next album. Instead, Jimmy Buffett was given the song, and it launched his career.

A few months later, my third grade teacher Diane Rooks at Central Primary asked my class to read a book and deliver a report. There was a catch, however. We had to give the report as a speech in front of the class. Furthermore, we had to dress up like the main character.

As I scanned the books in the school library, I finally found the perfect book. It was a children's biography on Elvis.

On the day of the report, my mother dressed me in white pants, a big belt, gold sunglasses and sent me to school with an Elvis album in my hand.

After I gave my presentation, I asked the class if they wanted to hear a song. I shook my hips and lip synced "Jailhouse Rock" and "Hound Dog," as Mrs. Rooks spun the records. A few of the girls screamed at me. For a day, I was a third grade rock star.

"Elvis! Elvis!" shouted some girls at me as I walked through the playground to the monkey bars.

"THANKYOUVERYMUCH!" I replied in the voice of the King.

Twenty years later, I made my first visit to Graceland. After viewing the gold piano, Jungle Room, and his private jet, I realized it was good to be the King.

Elvis would have turned seventy-five this year. It's hard to imagine him in his seventies. Would he still be performing? Acting in movies? Doing Weight Watchers commercials on television?

A few weeks ago, I took my mother to lunch. The last few years have been challenging to watch Alzheimer's take control of her mind.

I asked her as we rode to lunch, "Momma, do you want me to play any music?"

"Do you have any Elvis?" she asked.

As "Don't Be Cruel" played on my car stereo, I looked over and she was singing every word, note for note. She even clapped her hands.

Alzheimer's may take away her memories. It may take away her ability to speak. It may take away her ability to sing.

But it can't take away the King.

BYLINES FROM SELMA

Southern Spice, *Times-Georgian,* January 18, 2015

———

S omewhere between "Georgia on My Mind" and a typewriter there was a little magic.

As music filled the room, I stood close by watching Joe Cumming smile as his fingers hit the black and white keys of his grand piano. Here, standing beside him, his wife of sixty-six years, Emily, hummed the tune while he instructed me with a short piano lesson.

"You've got to incorporate more of the black keys in your playing," Joe urged me. "The piano sounds better when you play both the black and white keys. Just listen to the old classics, jazz and gospel tunes."

A retired professor from the University of West Georgia, Joe Cumming has never quit teaching. While I looked at his fingers, I realized they've been making beautiful music for most of his life. And they've touched much more than just the keys of a piano.

Before he became a professor, for twenty-eight years Cumming worked as a reporter for *Newsweek's* Atlanta bureau.

"*Newsweek* bureau chief Bill Emerson hired me in 1957 as the civil rights movement was beginning to take shape," said Cumming. "I think I realized the magnitude of this early on because I had majored in history, and this was falling in line. I remember saying to myself, 'This is history.'"

It didn't take long before Joe realized something incredible was developing when he heard the voice of the movement's rising star fill a room.

"He had a rhythm," said Cumming. "His rhetoric and delivery were different. He spoke from the heart. Martin Luther King Jr. had something special."

Through the next few years, Cumming and King would cross paths many times.

"He was a complicated fellow, and I couldn't help but admire him," said Cumming. "He was a real major figure, but he wasn't like a big shot. He had a sweetness about him and was driven from within. And he was always straightforward."

In the early 1960s, many media outlets began to give the impression that King's ideology was advocating a turn towards Communism or the Muslim movement. In a letter written to Joe Cumming on December 22, 1961, archived at Atlanta's King Center, Dr. King argued the misinterpretations and inaccuracies of such accusations.

"Such an idea is so far out of harmony with my general thinking that I am sure some people will wonder why I take the time to answer it," King wrote. "Suffice it to say that I can see no greater tragedy befalling the Negro than a turn to either Communism or Black Nationalism as a way out of the present dilemma … I have always contended that we as a race must not seek to rise from a position of disadvantage to one of advantage, thus subverting justice. Our aim must always be to create a moral balance in society where democracy and brotherhood will be a reality for all men."

For the next few years, the movement continued to grow stronger with the Freedom Rides, integration of colleges and universities, the March on Washington and eventually the passage of the Civil Rights Act of 1964 that banned discrimination based on "race, color, religion, sex, or national origin" in employment practices and public accommodations.

However, the movement was far from finished. When a group undertook an ambitious voter registration program in Selma, Alabama, it was met in the face of opposition from Selma's sheriff, Jim Clark. That led to the march from Selma to the state capital in Montgomery.

On March 7, 1965, more than six hundred peaceful protestors began the march when they were met at the Edmund Pettus Bridge with state troopers and local law enforcement officers. In an event popularly known as "Bloody Sunday," the protestors were attacked with tear gas, billy clubs, rubber tubes wrapped in barbed wire, and bull whips.

The national news footage from this event provoked a national response. Two weeks later, the marchers obtained a court order permitting them to make the march without incident.

"I covered the march for *Newsweek*, walked many miles and spent a few nights with the group," Cumming said, who later was promoted to southern bureau chief and chronicled some of his stories in his book *Bylines*, published in 2010. "We were surrounded by the National Guard and one night I was with King and he wanted to go out. He needed to go to the bathroom.

"When we walked up to the building where he would logically go, one of his assistants asked the guard if he could go through to use the restroom," continued Cumming. "The guard was very ugly about it and said he couldn't go through. King walked away and looked at me and said very nonchalantly with a smile, 'Well, he didn't have to be so nasty about it.' It was a really quaint moment. He was very calm. He wasn't angry."

And Cumming said he wasn't afraid as a white journalist because the magnitude of history was unfolding.

"I was threatened very little," said Cumming. "We would occasionally get smears from the crowd, but mostly we were usually left alone to be reporters. I caught a little roughness on the sidelines from Klansman types, but I wasn't bothered much."

Eight days after the march began, President Lyndon Johnson delivered a televised speech in support for a voting rights bill.

"But even if we pass this bill, the battle will not be over," said Johnson. "What happened in Selma is part of a far larger movement which reaches into every section and state of America. It is the effort of American Negroes to secure for themselves the full blessings of American life.

"Their cause must be our cause, too," continued Johnson. "Because it is not just Negroes, but really it is all of us, who must overcome the crippling legacy of bigotry and injustice. And we shall overcome."

A few months later the Voting Rights Act of 1965 was passed.

"One of the criticisms I have of the new movie *Selma* is I don't think it's right to belittle Lyndon Johnson," said Cumming. "Without him getting on board and passing the Voting Rights Act and Civil Rights Act, blacks would still be regarded as not fully human people. He told his constituents that the Democrats would lose the South for the next ten years, but it was the right thing to do. He changed the whole scheme of things and LBJ deserves that credit."

And Joe Cumming had a ringside seat.

"The Civil Rights Movement was the greatest gift from my guardian angel because I had a free ticket to whole thing," said Cumming. "In one interview between just me and Martin Luther King, I realized he was a real person talking. He wasn't a politician. The effect of what he said was 'Why me? But I guess I am the one that has to be.' Although he loved the attention, he would have been happy not to be the one.

"King was a thoughtful man," continued Cumming. "He knew he was doing something big. It was clear he realized he was called. When he spoke to the public, he spoke from the heart."

Perhaps King said it best when he closed his 1961 letter to Cumming.

"May I say in conclusion that the Negro is American in culture, language, and loyalty, and I am convinced that the vast majority of us will continue to struggle with the weapons of love and nonviolence to establish a better social order," wrote King. "I only advocate adhering to an ideology as old as the insights of Jesus of Nazareth and as meaningful as the techniques of Mohandas K. Gandhi."

As issues of racial violence and hatred continue throughout our land in towns like Ferguson, Missouri, a new level of awareness is rising. The Civil Rights Movement brought a new consciousness that enveloped a society to embrace a minority race as fully human. Like Jesus and Gandhi, Dr. Martin Luther King Jr. was murdered. Yet, like Jesus and Gandhi, he also changed the world.

And he did it "in the name of love."

A SEPTEMBER DRIVE

Southern Spice, *Times-Georgian*, September 1, 2013

———

I miss the bus ride—that moment of stepping aboard dressed in my football pants, T-shirt, and cleats while walking past pretty cheerleaders shaking pom-poms in the air.

Whether our destination was Cedartown, Calhoun, or Lafayette, it didn't matter. We were destined for another battle under the lights on a Friday night.

There was always an escort led by officers Aubrey Mitchell, Willie North, and Michael Mansour of the Carrollton Police Department. A caravan of parents formed a convoy behind us as Carrollton High Band Director Don Hall loaded his group of musicians, flag twirlers, and majorettes in a nearby parking lot. For a moment, there was nothing better than the call of the road.

Silence filled the bus rides to the game until the giggles of cheerleaders echoed from the second row. The scent of our field house locker room always tagged along as the smell of tobacco spit drifted from a coach's styrofoam cup.

And here we were once again on the road. Another town, another opponent, another stadium—within a few hours we would snap our chin straps and prepare to huddle before a referee summoned us on the field.

Once we arrived at our destination, we quickly grabbed our helmets and shoulder pads and walked to our visiting locker room. The cheerleaders carried their banners and signs as the coaches tested the walkie-talkies and headsets they would later use to navigate the play calling.

There's something special about walking into a stadium for the first time. Just to walk the field before the game to see if the grass was an inch taller than our home turf or even find an occasional rock or small dirt patch that may make a difference should the score come down to the wire.

The time we endured from arriving at our destination to the high pitch of the first whistle seemed to last forever. Eventually, we began our pregame drills—going through the motions of running, catching, kicking, tackling, and punting. And then it was time. It was time to huddle for the last moment in the locker room hoping your name would be called in the starting lineup.

After a few words and thoughts from Coach Charlie Grisham, we lined up to run down the sidelines in front of our hometown fans, as the marching band formed a tunnel with cheerleaders holding a huge banner.

Within a few seconds of reaching the end zone, the drum major raised her hands to lead the band in our fight song, as we ripped the big banner and jumped together on the sidelines, as the crowd cheered with pride. Coach Grisham told us to "give it all we got" and then led us in the Lord's Prayer.

Finally, it was time for the kicker to put his toe to the leather and let the game begin.

After all the hours in the weight room, practicing two times per day in the muggy August heat with blisters on my toes and an aching neck, I was ready. After lining up in what seemed like a thousand practice drills, while dodging shin splints and hip pointers, it was time to put it all together. It was time to play at your best level, even if meant the possibility of an opposing player knocking you to the ground. And for the next few hours, all of the hard work we endured became worth every single second to play a game.

Once again, football season has arrived. Every once in a while, I still long to suit up and tackle someone, but then the pain I sometimes feel in my lower back from a football injury reminds me I'm not seventeen years old anymore. The pain will remain with me for the rest of my life, but yet I ask, "Would I do it all over again?" And without a moment's hesitation I answer, "You better believe I would."

There's no doubt to take a risk is to embrace the very best of life. That's what I love about football. That's why I played the game.

STRETCHING CLASS

Southern Spice, *Times-Georgian*, December 7, 2014

———

I can touch my toes again.

And it hasn't come easy. Perhaps it's from too much sitting or a love affair with fried chicken, but something happened a few years ago, when I turned forty.

"I know the feeling," said Carrollton orthopedic surgeon Greg Slappey. "My body has started hurting in places it used to not hurt. There's a reason why most professional athletes retire in their midthirties. Flexibility is extremely important after the age of forty."

For the last few years my flexibility has been in decline (and I've exercised more in my forties than I did in my twenties and thirties combined).

"It will get worse unless you take care of yourself," reassured Dr. Slappey. "You need to stretch every day."

Recently, I decided to start a disciplined workout regime. I awoke at 5:00 a.m. and took every class the gym offered at 5:30. For the first few days, I felt energized before sunrise. Within two weeks, my body hurt so bad I had to stop exercising.

"I can't even touch my toes," I complained to my wife. "My body is so stiff I struggled to tie my shoes this morning."

"You need to try yoga," she said. "It's great for your back and flexibility. You should go with me sometimes."

After a few days, I finally told her I'd go with her.

"Can I call it 'Stretching Class' instead of 'Yoga'?" I asked.

"Just get over it," she replied. "There's always at least one male in the yoga classes. Now there will be two. Please don't be offended if I set up on the other side of the studio. I'm not sure I can watch you do this and not laugh."

"Thanks," I replied. "I love you, too."

Upon arrival at a local yoga studio, I unrolled my mat and smiled at my wife who was already laughing. Within a few minutes, our instructor began to lead the class as I stretched up, down, sideways, and more. It didn't take long to realize I was stretching parts of my body I didn't know existed.

After fifty minutes of putting my hips, arms, and legs in positions named after animals (*downward dog, scared cat, reverse eagle* and *cow pose*), Kendra instructed the class to lie flat on our backs and relax for the last ten minutes. She even gave us a bath cloth that had been dipped in something that smelled like Vick's salve.

Suddenly, I became the guy like Mikey on the old Quaker Oats Life cereal commercial.

I liked it. And I felt great.

For years, I've stereotyped yoga to be an exercise where people put their legs over their heads, burned incense, and chanted funny noises. What I discovered was the complete opposite. Yoga is more like Carrollton coaching-legend Charlie Grisham's pregame warm-up stretches than an act at Cirque du Soleil.

"Garrett, you're the most inflexible player I've ever coached," Grisham once shouted at me during football practice.

And if there's any way Coach Grisham was watching me from above while I attempted yoga, there's no doubt he would still say the same thing.

Oh well, say what you want. At least I can touch my toes again.

I CALLED HIM CHACHI

Southern Spice, *Times-Georgian*, April 26, 2015

———

I took the dare.

And that's the truth. As I sat with a group of coworkers inside the press box at Sanford Stadium eating a pregame meal, we marveled at the celebrity in our presence.

Even though legendary Georgia Bulldog play-by-play announcer Larry Munson stood close by with the clock ticking away before going on the air, he was overshadowed by another celebrity.

"Look who just walked into the room," said my friend Graham Edwards. "Does anyone recognize that guy?"

"Isn't that Scott Baio?" said my friend Jack Calhoun.

It was. During the 1970s and '80s, one of the most popular television shows was *Happy Days.* The ABC sitcom introduced the world to Ritchie and Joanie Cunningham, Potsie Weber, Ralph Malph, and the one and only Arthur Fonzarelli, also known as Fonzie or the Fonz.

In the show's fourth season, Baio joined the cast as Fonzie's cousin Chachi Arcola. And here he was in our presence.

"Who's up for the challenge?" declared my friend Mike Mobley. "I dare one of you to walk up to him and call him Chachi."

"I'll do it," I quickly replied.

It was 1987 and since I was the newcomer to the student assistant staff of the University of Georgia Sports Communications Office, I stepped up to the challenge.

As Baio stood at a counter preparing to eat a stadium hot dog, I walked up to him and held out my hand and said with a big smile— "Chachi! Is that you Chachi?"

He was not amused.

"No," he replied. "It's Scott. Scott Baio."

"I'm Joe—Joe Garrett," I replied. "Chachi, I mean Scott, I'm a big fan. I just couldn't help but call you Chachi because of the years I watched you on *Happy Days*."

Again, he was not amused, and he walked away.

Little did I know that Baio would be the first of many celebrity encounters I would have. It's one thing to see a famous person when you pay to see a play or concert. It's another thing to encounter a celebrity in everyday life.

For someone growing up in New York City or Los Angeles, this is perhaps a frequent occurrence. For someone from this neck of the woods, however, it's a rare opportunity.

A few years ago, Jimmy Buffett munched on a cheeseburger a few tables away from me and my wife at the Buckhead Diner. Barbara Walters walked into Le Cirque where my wife and I dined one night in New York City. Even former teen idol and star of *The Partridge Family* David Cassidy sat next to us at dinner one evening at Lago Mar in Ft. Lauderdale.

And then there was the legendary Gene Simmons of the rock group KISS who walked onto my elevator at the Plaza Hotel in Manhattan, football announcer and Kathie Lee's husband Frank Gifford standing behind me waiting for a cab in Boston, President Jimmy Carter's mother, Lillian, walking beside me at a Braves game, best-selling author Pat Conroy strolling along the sidewalk in Highlands, North Carolina, Lewis Grizzard ordering a hot dog at the concession stand at Ole Miss, Wolfman Jack boarding an airplane, Lionel Richie walking through security behind me at the Atlanta airport, Baseball Hall of Famer Bobby Cox washing his hands in the men's restroom in Orlando, and Sharon Stone sitting on a beach in Ft. Lauderdale wearing a bikini.

It even runs in my family. My brother once sat next to Paul Newman in a Chicago restaurant where a group of women dropped and broke a bottle of wine on the floor and Newman helped them clean the spill. My mother encountered Hershel Walker sitting on a park bench in Athens, Georgia, Heather Locklear sunbathing next to her at a hotel pool in Savannah, and Sylvester Stallone checking out from a Florida hotel.

"Herschel was so well-mannered and signed an autograph for me, and Sylvester Stallone just nodded his head when I smiled at him," said my mother. "And Heather Locklear was so nice. She liked the color of my hair."

Even my wife and one of her friends laughed with two old men who flirted with them while waiting for a table at the Loveless Café outside Nashville.

"When we walked to our table, someone stopped us and asked us if we knew who we were talking to," said my wife Ali. "It was Grandpa Jones from *Hee Haw* and Goober from *The Andy Griffith Show*."

Who knows who'll be next? Maybe a US president, famous singer or even one of Charlie's "Angels" will make the list. But if I ever cross paths with Scott Baio again, I know what I'm going to do. I'm going to take the dare.

Oh yeah, I'm going to call him "Chachi."

DINNER ON THE GROUND

Southern Spice, *Times-Georgian,* April 29, 2012

B owdon women know how to cook.

I know this because I've eaten their food. Unfortunately, it took the death of my dad's first cousin Hugh Ayers to eat this incredible meal.

It wasn't served at a restaurant. It was served in the basement of Bowdon First United Methodist Church an hour before Hugh was eulogized.

On the morning of the funeral my dad called and asked me if I wanted to go eat with the family at the church.

"Some of the women at the church are preparing the meal," he said. "They're going to do a covered dish."

Quicker than you can say "cracklin' cornbread," I replied with a quick "Yes."

Covered dish meals are a staple of southern culture. I don't know where the first covered dish or "dinner on the ground" was served, but I wouldn't be surprised if it has roots somewhere between the Georgia communities of Victory and Burwell.

I once attended a business conference where a motivational speaker asked the audience, "How do you want to be eulogized?"

I don't really worry about my eulogy since I can't control what people may say anyway. I only hope there's a covered-dish lunch so everyone can eat well.

As I stood in line to wait for my turn at the food table, I strategized how I was going to fit so much food on one plate. Casseroles, roast beef, ham, homemade rolls, hot jalepeno cornbread, homemade mac 'n' cheese, green beans, peas, and sweet potatoes with brown sugar on top adorned the long table. Homemade cakes, cookies, and pies awaited at the end.

"I hope you don't mind if I get a little bite of each dessert?" I asked one of the women who prepared the food.

"Honey, you just get as much as you want," she replied. "Go get you one of the big plates if you want."

The last time I was in New York City I had to walk past one of Donald Trump's buildings every morning to attend my business meeting. Trump once told a reporter he eats at the finest restaurants in the world.

I'm sure he does.

However, on this day, the folks at Bowdon Methodist served me a five-star covered-dish meal. I didn't even have to walk past a Trump building to get there. I turned left at the main intersection's red light in the town known as the "Friendly City."

Hugh Ayers lived a full life.

He was a military hero, husband, father, former tax assessor, professional bridge player, and, at one time, owned the largest poultry farm in the state of Georgia. On the day everyone honored him, his family gathered together to eat a covered-dish meal.

I hate Hugh wasn't there.

SERVING TIME

Southern Spice, *Times-Georgian*, March 23, 2014

———

H e was buck naked in the library.
Within minutes of the police arriving, this individual wearing nothing but a smile had locked himself in one of the study rooms at the college library. As the police knocked on the door, he refused to open it and then tried to catch himself on fire. Let's just say he wasn't a "hunk of burning love."

Eventually, the door was opened and a blanket covered the naked man. And so began my adventure of listening to a case as a member of the Carroll County Grand Jury.

Several years ago, I was drafted to listen to ninety-eight cases on a $25 per day salary. It was the first time I had ever served on a jury. After hearing stories like the naked man and so many others for three days, I would have gladly paid the government $25 a day in lieu of my salary for this type of entertainment.

We had a solid group who listened closely to determine whether a trial was necessary. My longtime friend and former Carrollton City Schools Superintendent Tom Upchurch sat next to me for the three days. He was elected foreman, and he quickly appointed me assistant foreman, which meant I had to do all of the work.

Since we knew about half of the people in the ninety-eight cases, we had to often recuse ourselves from voting. It didn't matter because in between we listened to stories about peeping Toms, love triangles in a local neighborhood, and disputes about dogs barking too loudly.

You can't make this stuff up.

The majority of the cases involved serious issues that needed to move to the next level. After hearing a string of cases that broke our hearts, all of the sudden a really good one interrupted the monotony.

"This individual has a long history of breaking into homes," said the assistant district attorney. "He's served time for his past arrests for theft."

Whether it was the fourth or fifth time the individual had been arrested, he obviously picked the wrong time to have his case before a grand jury.

"Does anyone have any affiliation with this individual?" the assistant DA asked the jury. "If so, please leave the room before the vote."

Within a second, Upchurch raised his hand.

"Unfortunately, I have an affiliation with this burglar," said Upchurch. "I was his first victim in 1987. Ask him if he still has my watch I never got back after he broke into my house through the back porch window."

In case you're wondering, the burglar had to go to trial.

And after ninety-eight cases, we were exhausted but thankful for our time to experience how our judicial system operates.

I hope the love triangles and peeping Toms resolved their issues. As for the naked man in the library, maybe he bought some new clothes. Maybe he's found peace within, and perhaps has joined the nudist colony outside the Burwell cemetery.

But most of all—I hope he's working out at the gym. If you're going to strip naked in a public library, it's important to look your best.

PEANUT POWER

Southern Spice, *Times-Georgian*, August 23, 2015

We left Plains, Georgia, with a T-shirt in our hands. On the shirt was an iron-on picture of a James Earl Carter headshot inside a giant peanut. Below the peanut read the inscription "Peanut Power." It was 1976, and as the nation celebrated a bicentennial birthday, a Georgia peanut farmer vied for the highest job in the land.

And he did it with a smile.

Before we passed by his brother Billy's gas station on the way out of the tiny Georgia town no bigger than Roopville, my brothers and I put on our new shirts.

"Y'all take care of those Jimmy Carter shirts," my mother demanded. "If he wins, y'all can wear them when we go to Washington, D.C., next summer."

And we did.

Throughout our nation's history, individuals have toured the White House dressed in their sharpest attire from tuxedos to their Sunday best. As for the Garrett boys, we walked through the east entrance of the White House in 1977 wearing our "Peanut Power" T-shirts.

"We're from Georgia," my mother told everyone from the security guard to our tour guide. "Jimmy grew up just two and half hours from our hometown."

Folks from Georgia beamed with pride as one of our own had become the president of the United States.

It was a different time. Democrats and Republicans may have disagreed on issues, but the rhetoric between political parties was quite cordial compared to today.

The nation, still scarred from Richard Nixon's resignation following the Watergate scandal, longed for an honest politician who would tell them the truth. And that's what Jimmy Carter promised this country.

"I'll never tell a lie," promised Carter. "I'll never make a misleading statement. I'll never betray the confidence that any of you had in me. And I'll never avoid a controversial issue."

Carter's legacy has suffered due to his political enemies, but he's dedicated his life to service and to a strong commitment to bring peaceful resolutions to a very complex world.

"War may sometimes be a necessary evil," said Carter. "But no matter how necessary, it is always an evil, never a good. We will not learn how to live together in peace by killing each other's children."

Last week, Jimmy Carter informed the world he has an aggressive form of cancer that's spread throughout his body. At ninety years old, his time is perhaps limited.

Hopefully, his strong desire to bring peace to the world will outweigh his shortcomings during his presidency. I have a strong feeling history will treat him with kindness.

"For I know the thoughts that I think toward you," writes Jeremiah. "Thoughts of peace and not of evil, to give you a future and a hope."

That's how I'll remember Jimmy Carter. He has lived the words of Jeremiah. He is never afraid to get his hands dirty and face opposition. He is an advocate for peace. He is a giant towards helping the hungry, poor, and oppressed. And the small-town peanut farmer from Georgia is always bigger than politics.

That's real power.

Joe (left), brother Bill (right) and mom Betty in Washington D.C. 1977.

AN OPEN TALK

Southern Spice, *Times-Georgian,* July 5, 2015

———

For a few seconds, the room was silent.

My friend Thomas made an announcement during a retreat I attended as a board member for a nonprofit organization. It was unexpected, but the group of eleven individuals from different walks of life listened intently when he said—"I'm gay."

It was the first time Thomas had revealed a secret he'd been living with for almost forty years. He felt close enough to our group to finally break his silence.

Since most of us had worked closely as board members for the previous two years, I never thought of him as gay or straight. He was a hard worker, excellent with numbers, and a great presenter, who displayed a level of toughness when we faced a controversial decision the previous year.

But for the first time in my life, I was actually present when someone broke his silence. The next day, Thomas shattered every stereotype I was taught to believe about people who are gay.

"Believe it or not, I have a friend who's convinced someone he went to school with turned out gay because his mother made him take piano lessons as a child," I told him.

"Joe, you could dress all your sons in tutus, high heels, and makeup, and it wouldn't turn them gay," Thomas said.

"Oh sure, they would be picked on—but my point is it's not something I chose. But look at today's world with professional football players and other athletes coming out—has their sexuality impaired their performance? It was nothing my parents did. I realized at a young age that I was different. And by the time I was a teenager—I realized I was gay.

"I tried to hide it by dating girls," he continued. "All I wanted was to feel normal, to fit in and not face the disgrace and ridicule of a society who looked down upon us as evil creatures."

"So you're not evil like that television evangelist proclaimed on television last night," I joked.

"Well, seriously, for some people who read certain Biblical verses literally, specifically Leviticus 20:13—I'll always be viewed as evil and treated as though I'm not fully human," Thomas said. "But keep in mind there are texts from the very same Bible which were used for centuries by various groups to support slavery, women as subhuman creatures and decry abomination for anyone getting a divorce. There's even a text in the twenty-first chapter of Deuteronomy that advises parents to have their child stoned to death if their son doesn't obey them and listen to them. Now how many people would still be alive if we still supported that text?"

"How does your family treat you?" I asked.

"Some better than others," said Thomas. "My sister still will not let me be around her children because she doesn't want her children to think they condone my 'lifestyle.' Joe, my lifestyle is that I wake up every day, get dressed, fix a cup of coffee, and go to work. I like to watch football games, go to church, volunteer in the community, eat great meals, and do basically everything most human beings like to do. The only difference is I'd rather share my life with a man just like you want to share yours with a woman.

"It's the way I was born," continued Thomas. "It's the way God made me. I know I'll never be considered normal by some people—I only want to be treated fully as a human being."

Recently, one of my friends ranted over our society's culture shift when he argued: "Thomas Jefferson was a Christian and a Founding Father, he helped draft the words to guide our country based on Christian values and teachings," my friend insisted. "All we have to do is look at God's word and it tells us very clearly that homosexuality is evil."

After my conversation, I decided to read Jefferson's words, which contradict my friend's assertion. They can be found in a document called the *Declaration of Independence.*

"We hold these truths to be self-evident, that all men are created equal, that they are endowed by their Creator with certain unalienable Rights, that among these are Life, Liberty and the pursuit of Happiness," Jefferson wrote.

I'm sure the debates will continue to rage on. They do when a new level of tolerance is emerging. As the "times are a-changing," the more I learn—the more I realize how much I don't know. But one thing I feel confident about is—love will prevail. It never loses.

This I know.

WEARING THE BADGE

Southern Spice, *Times-Georgian*, November 25, 2012

I used to wear Granddaddy's badge.

After I ate my grandmother's breakfast of hot biscuits with bacon and sausage, I would put on my pretend law enforcement uniform before strapping on a holster with a fake pistol to go fight the bad guys. Although my grandparents gave me the freedom to search for imaginary criminals in their backyard, I was monitored closely. It wasn't for my safety—but for the safety of the badge.

My grandfather's badge wasn't a twenty-five-cent toy purchased at a five-and-dime store, but a real Carroll County sheriff's badge. From 1953 to 1957, my grandfather Leonas Garrett served as the sheriff of Carroll County.

I've always felt a connection to sheriffs. Whether it was Sheriff Andy Taylor, Sheriff Buford Pusser, Sheriff Wyatt Earp, or Sheriff Buford T. Justice, these men who wear the badge represent law and order.

"Having a good sheriff is like having a twelve-pack and a bag of Krystal burgers," said my friend David Hughes from Dawsonville, who specializes in eating doughnuts with law enforcement officials. "They always provide comfort on a rowdy Saturday night."

Times have changed. While current Carroll County Sheriff Terry Langley and his deputies chase all of the problems in our society today, my grandfather made sure all of the town drunks sobered on a Saturday night, so they could make it to church the next morning. Like the fictional town of Mayberry, Carroll County had its share of Otis Campbells in the 1950s.

"Most of the inmates were local men who seemed to get in trouble on the weekends," said my father, Jimmy Garrett. "Besides, going to the Carroll County jail wasn't so bad because my mother used to cook for the prisoners, and I would run errands to pick up cigarettes and Prince Albert in a can for them."

As I said earlier, times have changed.

I've read most of the classic works of Shakespeare, Hemingway, Steinbeck, and F. Scott Fitzgerald, but, when it comes to pure entertainment, nothing beats a good cop television show. Recently, my good friend Matt Webb, who is a bounty hunter in Louisiana, was featured on the television show *Big Easy Justice*.

"As a bounty hunter, we get to kick down the door," said Webb. "The adrenaline level is through the roof. Last weekend we caught the biggest heroin dealer in New Orleans."

"Why don't you try bird or deer hunting?" I asked. "It's a lot safer."

"That's too boring," said Webb. "Birds and deer don't shoot back."

So, here's to those who wear the badge and catch the bad guys. May you continue to protect and serve our communities throughout the land. Don't forget when you come home it's OK to allow little boys and girls to wear your badge for a little while.

You may inspire them to become a writer.

Joe with grandfather Leonas 1973

Will with grandfather Jimmy Garrett 2011

STILL WITH MAGILL

Southern Spice, *Times-Georgian,* August 31, 2014

I saw him numerous times with a broom and trash bag.

He took pride in cleanliness. He always wanted things to look their absolute best. Whether it was a candy wrapper on the ground or a small weed sprouting near a tree, he demanded his headquarters always look impeccably groomed.

It's the little things that matter. Thirty-four years after becoming the tennis coach at the University of Georgia, Dan Magill retired in 1988 as the winningest coach in NCAA Division I tennis history, with 706 wins leading the Bulldogs to 21 SEC outdoor and indoor titles and national championships in 1985 and '87.

He grew up in Athens, Georgia, hanging around the athletic fields at UGA. After graduating from his beloved hometown alma mater, he served in the United States Marine Corps during World War II. Once he returned from the war, he turned his eyes on his two loves—journalism and sports.

Magill served as the prep sports editor for the *Atlanta Journal* where he became a master promoter of high school sporting events. He loved tennis so much that in the 1940s he put together a tennis match between Jack Kramer and Bobby Riggs, which drew three thousand people, the largest tennis crowd in the Southeast at the time.

Those skills would play into his hiring as the sports information director at UGA in 1949. In 1954, he expanded his duties when he became the school's tennis coach. Since he was an assistant athletic director at the time, Magill decided to hire himself for the coaching job.

He has been called by many the "greatest Bulldog of all." Last Sunday, at the age of 93, Magill died in Athens.

In the fall of 1987, I was hired as a student assistant by current UGA Senior Associate Athletic Director Claude Felton. My primary duty involved working with Magill. My secondary duty was to always refer to Georgia Tech as "The Enemy" in Magill's presence.

For the next several months, Magill taught me how to become a writer, a statistician, a promoter, and anything it took to elevate the UGA tennis program and fill the seats at Henry Feild Stadium. And filling the seats he mastered, often drawing larger crowds than basketball and baseball games. He was a master storyteller, and his incredible brain could recall sports scores and events faster than any computer today.

"Coach, were you this smart when you were in school?" I once asked him.

"I was because I sat next to 'A-Plus Mason' and 'Straight-A Milligan,'" he replied. "I always picked good seats."

He proclaimed himself as the world's fastest two-finger typist.

"He was," said Carrollton native Mark Parkman, who worked alongside Magill while he was a student at UGA. "He actually made the *Guinness Book of World Records* for two things—the fastest two-finger typist (148 words per minute) and the longest table tennis point (118 minutes in 1936)."

Magill threw me into the fire pit of journalism and marketing. If I wrote (what I thought was) a good story, he ripped it apart and challenged me to make it better. If the Georgia tennis team's match against a good school didn't make the front sports page of *The Athens Banner-Herald* or *The Red & Black*, he challenged me to schmooze the editors so it never happened again.

He demanded excellence. And I'll forever be grateful for his high expectations. But, most of all, I'll remember him for his wit and his incredible southern accent.

"In Magill, you have South-in-the-mouth that is matchless," wrote the late Lewis Grizzard in his book *Don't Sit Under the Grits Tree with Anyone Else but Me.* "Suffice it to say, Magill's 'great' is not 'grate,' but 'greyette.' His 'coach' is more 'co-atch.'"

When I first met Grizzard at a book signing, who also worked with Magill while he was a UGA student, I told him about working for our mutual friend.

"Dan taught me everything I know," Grizzard said with a big grin.

One even considered himself lucky when Magill uttered the words "pretty gurl" in his presence or offered you a "Co-Cola."

It's hard to believe his presence will no longer be a part of the landscape on the UGA campus, but his legacy will forever shine. For four years, I took numerous classes from geology to business law. Although I'm grateful for a diploma that hangs on my wall, I must confess that Dan Magill taught me more than any class I took.

Magill often made speeches to local civic clubs and occasionally would ask me to listen to them while he practiced. He always began each speech with the words, "My fellow Georgia Bulldogs, chosen people of the Western world."

His tribal mentality towards college athletics was quite comical, but his contribution to so many was quite vast. As college football is once again underway, I'll often think about his love of the Bulldogs.

I hope Georgia wins many games, but most of all, come November 29, I hope we once again play a great game for Magill and defeat the Enemy.

A PRAYER IN JORDAN-HARE

Southern Spice, *Times-Georgian*, December 1, 2013

———

(An open letter to my sons)

Dear Sons:

A couple of weeks ago, I watched an improbable play from the upper deck at Jordan-Hare Stadium in Auburn, Alabama. With the game on the line, the Georgia Bulldogs orchestrated one of the greatest comebacks in the history of a rivalry that spans 121 years. The Bulldogs scored 21 points to come from behind to take the lead 38 to 37 with just 1:49 on the clock.

Auburn was stuck as it faced fourth down, and it looked like the game belonged to Georgia.

That's when Auburn quarterback Nick Marshall threw a Hail Mary pass. The ball appeared to be knocked down by two Georgia defenders, but instead it was tipped into the hands of Auburn's Ricardo Louis who ran to the end zone, as the crowd erupted. The game appeared to be over, but Georgia still had twenty-five seconds to retake the lead.

It would not happen.

This game will forever be remembered as "The Prayer in Jordan-Hare," but I'll remember it for something else. I'll remember it for Georgia trailing 20 points with less than 11 minutes left in the game. I'll remember it for Georgia quarterback Aaron

Murray never quitting and leading the charge for the Bulldogs to drive to the Auburn 20-yard-line as the clock expired.

I'll remember it because neither team ever quit.

Unfortunately, the Auburn Tigers won the game. Although I rooted for Georgia to win, I walked out of the stadium with a smile.

It was a heckuva football game.

Sometimes the game of football is compared to the game of life. Most of the comparisons are overrated. Football is a game. Life is much more difficult and complex. Occasionally, however, an important life lesson can be learned from the boys carrying the pigskin.

During halftime I stood along the exit ramp and watched hundreds of Georgia fans leave the stadium in disgust as Georgia trailed 27 to 10. Their faces looked like they received news their dog died. These fans had lost any hope of a comeback—did they not remember 1996?

There's no doubt the Georgia Bulldogs failed miserably during the first half. The team made many costly errors. Instead of focusing on the past, the team directed its focus to the second half.

During my senior year of high school, former Georgia state Senator Wayne Garner spoke to my class in an assembly held in the old Carrollton High School Auditorium.

"Be prepared to fail," Garner told our class. "Somewhere along the way, you're going to fail."

I had never heard someone say this before. My teachers made sure I learned the curriculum so I would pass each class. It may "be a sin to kill a mockingbird," but it was a bigger sin to ever fail a class in school.

Garner wasn't talking about school. He was talking about life.

"What's important is not your failure," Garner continued. "What's important is to put yourself out there and learn from your mistakes and grow from your experience."

In other words, it's OK to be wrong. It's not OK to stay wrong.

Each of you will choose a path. It probably won't be football, but whether it's architecture, business, medicine, ministry, technology or thousands of other possibilities—you'll be faced with many challenges.

Sometimes it's your soul's way of moving you in the right direction. Other times it's not.

Even though Aaron Murray and the Georgia Bulldogs lost the game, it doesn't make them losers. They didn't quit when most of their fans had given up. They believed in themselves when no one else did. That's just one of many keys to succeeding in life.

That's called hope. And as you grow older, you'll realize there's always hope even among the darkest of days.

Always give your very best. Hard work will always serve you well, but working smarter will carry you further. Be prepared to fall short even when you've given it your all.

Sometimes when you least expect it and you put yourself in the right position, the ball may bounce in your hands like that guy from Auburn.

So as the song says, "If someday the bases are loaded and they're counting on you/You just can't strike out if you'll up and shout/'Yabba-Dabba-Dabba,   Yabba-Dabba-Dabba/Yabba-Dabba-Dabba-Dabba-Doo.'"

Always the best,

Dad

RIDING WITH THE DEVIL

Southern Spice, *Times-Georgian*, October 25, 2015

I ran into the devil, and he took me for a ride.

We didn't meet at the crossroads. If my memory serves me correctly, he picked me up at my house in a pickup truck. My mother told me to make sure he didn't keep me out too late.

"Y'all are too old for this," she yelled at my friend, who had recently turned sixteen, as I entered his vehicle.

We were on our way to pick up the werewolf.

Mom was probably right. We were too old to be trick or treating. But my friend had a crush on a girl, and he was too scared to call her. Dressed in his devil costume, however, he had no fear to go knock on her front door and ask for candy.

"What if her dad comes to the door and refuses to give us a treat?" I asked the devil.

"We'll park down the street so nobody in her family will see my truck," he replied. "He won't recognize us behind our masks."

After we picked up the werewolf, we rode around Carrollton for a while. While driving by Oak Grove Baptist Church, we saw a youth group gathered in a field. We couldn't tell if they were about to sing camp songs or play a game of "Red Rover, Red Rover—send Cindy right over."

"Let's turn the car around and go spook them," said the devil.

"Grrrrrrrrr," echoed the Werewolf.

My friend, the devil, had a voice where he could hit a high pitched laugh. As we again passed the group, the devil rolled down his window and laughed in a haunted voice as the teenagers looked stunned. He then "got a wheel" by spinning his tires to make a screech as we headed towards the next house to ask for candy.

We never returned to Oak Grove, but my guess is they did what good youth groups do—they prayed to keep the devil away.

A little while later, we arrived at the girl's home across town. And as the devil feared, the dad came to the door.

"Who are you?" he asked.

"I'm the devil," he replied with total confidence. "Is your daughter home?"

"No," the dad responded with a stone-cold poker face. "She's on a date with a guy at the movies."

The devil took off. And the werewolf and I, dressed as a creepy old man, were not too far behind.

Oh well, some things are not meant to be.

We live in a world today where some churches prohibit kids from wearing any type of scary costumes. Perhaps they're afraid of it bringing some type of evil into the psyche of these young children.

Sometimes I feel as if I'm Zorba the Greek laughing at the monks for such religious nonsense. Maybe it's time to let a little spooky fun back into Halloween.

Everything's going to be just fine.

And while I sit here today staring at a pumpkin outside my back door, I'm thinking of my friend, the werewolf. He grew up to become a pretty decent lawyer.

As for my friend, the devil—I know the prayers from the Oak Grove Baptist youth group worked that Halloween night in 1982.

He's now a preacher.

KINDERGARTEN CAGERS

Southern Spice, *Times-Georgian*, February 1, 2015

————

I t occurred two miles north of Roopville.
While the basketball world last week celebrated historic milestones of Coach Mike Krzyzewski's one thousandth career victory, the Atlanta Hawks' rise to become an NBA championship contender, and the West Georgia Wolves' winning season, a group of young boys chartered their own mark on the court.

"Let's score two," I said to the five- and six-year-old boys.

I've become a head coach for the first time. It wasn't a life-calling. I heard no voices from above whispering in my ear, "Thou shalt coach."

Instead, when I arrived home for lunch one day, my wife delivered the news.

"I called several of the moms in Henry's Oak Mountain Academy class, and we have enough boys to field a basketball team," she said.

"That's great," I replied. "They'll be a fun group to watch."

"Oh, you're going to be doing more than watching," she said. "I told everyone you'll be the coach."

Kids have a way of reigniting a spark in your life.

On the first day of practice, I couldn't wait to watch these kids dribble, shoot layups, and rebound like Shaquille O'Neal. But within the first two minutes of practice, I had an awakening.

Most of the kids, who are closer to age four than age six, looked at the basketball as if it was a foreign object.

Furthermore, I only had three kids who had developed the strength to actually shoot the ball higher than the net. And then as we started our first practice, the biggest surprise happened. Two of the players started crying.

"Everybody is genius," said Albert Einstein. "But if you judge a fish by its ability to climb a tree, it will live its whole life believing that it is stupid."

So, instead of shooting, we decided to learn to dribble. Then we learned how to pass, one step at a time—oh yes, one step at a time.

It's been said, "When the tide comes in, you can see who's been swimming naked."

Well, thankfully no one was naked, but my coaching skills were clearly on display as the season opened.

No one played his position correctly. The ball bounced over the players' heads. No points were scored. I wanted to look like coaching legends Dean Smith or John Wooden. Instead, I looked like a train wreck.

Even one of my players tugged on my shirt while he ran down the court.

"Can I go give my daddy a hug?" he asked.

He did.

For these past few weeks, the boys have kept dribbling, passing and trying to shoot. A few of them have learned their position and the zone defense.

In our most recent game it finally happened.

After challenging the boys to score two, they rose to the occasion in front of a packed house at Holy Ground Baptist Academy's gymnasium. After fighting hard for three quarters, one of the players took a pass, pivoted, shot the ball and scored two points.

We're all learning. And when the final whistle blows for the season, I suspect the parents will celebrate their sons' first experience with basketball. We'll remember the funny moments, their frustrations and the joy of watching our boys at such a young age. The focus on winning can come later in their lives.

As for today, we'll focus on something more. We'll give them all a hug.

A THANKSGIVING ROMANCE

Southern Spice, *Times-Georgian*, November 30, 2014

———

Harvey ate too much.

And so did Delores. For fifty-six years of marriage they always ate the same thing on Thanksgiving, except for this year. With all of their children scattered throughout the country, they decided to take the easy route. They ate their Thanksgiving meal at Cracker Barrel.

"Delores declared her oven was broken," said Harvey. "I knew better than to ask her if she was really serious, so I did what I've learned to do best after all these years. I shut up and didn't say a word. Then she told me I wasn't listening to her."

After the Macy's Thanksgiving Parade ended on television, Harvey and Delores boarded their 1998 Buick with 40,000 miles on the odometer and drove to Bremen. For the next twenty minutes, they talked about whether or not Cracker Barrel would have real dressing.

"I've never really understood what stuffing is," argued Delores. "It's supposed to be called 'dressing' where you make your biscuits and cornbread from scratch while you boil your hen before gathering your celery, onions, butter..."

By the time they reached Bowdon Junction, Delores was still describing how to make homemade dressing, while Harvey's mind began to wonder what time the Detroit Lions kicked off.

Within a few minutes, Harvey and Delores ordered the Thanksgiving special (a couple of slices of turkey breast, cornbread dressing, savory gravy, a sampling of sugar-cured ham, sweet potato casserole with pecans, cranberry relish, and a slice of pumpkin pecan streusel pie). After finishing their meal, they were too tired to tour the gift shop so they drove home where they could relax.

A few hours later, Harvey smelled a sweet aroma from the kitchen.

"What are you doing?" Harvey asked Delores, as he walked into the kitchen after waking up from his nap that began halfway through the fourth quarter of the Lions game.

"I'm making homemade dressing," she said. "And I'd appreciate it if you got out of the kitchen right now."

Harvey figured her oven was working again so he decided to walk outside and do what he does best. He piddled. For the next couple of hours, Harvey piddled around his carport before moving on to piddle in his yard.

When he walked back in the house, something smelled heavenly.

"I decided to make you that German chocolate cake you always liked," said Delores.

Harvey smiled and walked close to hug Delores when she demanded, "Not now. I told you you're in my way while I'm cooking. Now go back in the den and watch football."

Later that evening, Harvey and Delores enjoyed a delicious meal of dressing and cake. They both were still stuffed from their lunch at Cracker Barrel, but they found a way to keep eating.

For years, their Thanksgiving days were full-speed, balancing cooking a few dishes while getting their children bathed and dressed to visit relatives.

But that's been almost twenty-five years since they became empty nesters. On this Thanksgiving evening, they shared another homemade meal while Delores talked about what ingredients were missing in Cracker Barrel's dressing.

Once Harvey took a bite of Delores's cake, he complimented her cooking.

"I love you," he told Delores.

"I love you, too," she replied. "I'm tired and I'm ready to go to bed. Since I cooked, you can clean the kitchen. And don't forget to take out the trash and feed the neighbor's dog. They're still out of town. Good night, dear."

Delores went to bed. And Harvey ate another piece of cake.

PART III
WINTER

The world breaks everyone and afterward
many are strong in the broken places.

—ERNEST HEMINGWAY

A HEALING FIRE

Southern Spice, *Times-Georgian,* February 21, 2016

———

The fire crackled and snapped while I sipped my morning coffee. My dog sat close to my feet as the sun rose above the pines. Outside I heard the birds chirping in the breezy wind as I watched three cats chew on a squirrel's tail. For a moment I wondered, where is the rest of the squirrel? The little varmint probably didn't have a good night.

All was quiet in the house.

"Let us be silent, that we may hear—the whispers of God," wrote Ralph Waldo Emerson.

For a moment, the noise of a busy world could wait as I took another sip of coffee. The fire needed my attention. A poke here and a poke there and eventually another piece of wood transformed the room into a winter haven while my family slept.

When Don McLean sang "Bye bye, Miss American Pie," he declared "fire is the Devil's only friend." On this morning, however, I welcomed the flames.

And I saw no signs of the Devil.

It's hard to quiet the mind, especially in this technological world where I often feel the need to check my email or text messages every five minutes. Addiction is cruel. My iPhone is like crack (or so I'm told). On second thought, it's more like sitting at a blackjack table in Vegas, only it's not as much fun.

I long to return to the days when technology was simpler and life wasn't so fast paced. Perhaps it's time to pick up a book again, a real one with real paper and a spine. I think my Kindle will understand.

Within a few minutes, I began to realize my children would awaken. I poked at the fire. It started to rapidly burn and soon another piece of wood was needed.

Once again, it's hard to quiet the mind.

"There is calmness lived in a life of gratitude, a quiet joy," said Ralph H. Blum. "Sometimes you just need a break in a beautiful place. Alone to figure everything out."

After a while, I began to count a handful of life's blessings. The older I grow, the less I know. It's the mystery of living the questions.

Rarely do I close my eyes and ask God for favors anymore. I listen instead.

Some days I hear voices in my head. I feel ghosts on my shoulders. They're often cluttered and they disappear as quickly as they arrive, but every now and then a quiet whisper stops me in my tracks. It pushes me forward and not back.

There's a peace within sitting alone on a Sunday morning, while watching the flames flicker and feeling a dog cuddle at my feet. Within a few minutes, the sounds of little footsteps walking down the stairs will echo through the house. *Pitter patter. Pitter patter.*

One day they'll leave this nest and silence will permeate our home. Until then, I welcome the noise, the laughter, the chaos and all the highs and lows of rearing a household full of kids.

No matter what happens today or tomorrow, I realize life is going to be OK. God told me so as he warmed my soul through a healing fire.

A CHILD AT CHRISTMAS

West Georgia Living, December, 2014

———

He stood tall.

And no matter what the older kids said, he wasn't a doll. He was an action figure, all twelve inches of him.

Dressed in a red jumpsuit, he beat up all the bad guys and even once kissed a neighbor's Barbie doll. Ken didn't stand a chance when Steve Austin, the bionic Six Million Dollar Man, was around.

A few weeks before the bionic action figure arrived on Christmas morning, I sat on Santa's knee at the old downtown Rich's Department Store in Atlanta.

"I really want a Six Million Dollar Man action figure and a Stretch Armstrong," I told Santa. "Will you please think about bringing them to me? And if you can't fit them both in your bag, I'd rather have the Six Million Dollar Man."

"Have you been a good boy and nice to your parents, brothers, teachers, and friends?" Santa asked.

I halfway nodded my head. Santa smiled. I didn't have the courage to tell him how I bit my friend Joe Murrah in a backyard wrestling match the previous week.

But Santa delivered the Six Million Dollar Man anyway and even included Stretch Armstrong. I was grateful Santa brought gifts despite my shortcomings of mischief, biting and mimicking professional wrestlers on Saturday nights.

"Do you really think Santa looked into a snowball and saw me bite you and watched you put me in a headlock?" I asked Joe Murrah. "If he knows when we've been bad or good, how come he never mentioned it to me when I sat in his lap at Rich's. He brought us presents anyway."

"Santa didn't ask me either," said Joe Murrah. "But I asked for a Stretch Armstrong, too. And he didn't bring me one."

"I wonder if he thinks headlocks are really bad?"" I asked. "Maybe we should just stick to biting."

Of course, as we grew older we began to question Santa even more. Eventually, just like the characters in the children's book *The Polar Express*, we stopped hearing the jingle of Santa's sleigh bell.

But it was only for a few years. After my oldest son was born, the magic was back.

Maybe the Oak Ridge Boys say it best when they sing:

If it wasn't for kids have you ever thought
There wouldn't be a Santa Claus
Or look what the stork just brought
Thank God for kids
We'd all live in a quiet house
Without Big Bird or a Mickey Mouse
And Kool-Aid on the couch
Thank God for kids

The Christmas story remains forever engrained in my mind. As a child I learned about the pregnant Mary and her husband Joseph searching for a place of rest, only to find shelter in a rustic stable. As an adult, I'm learning Mary and Joseph's boy changed the world's consciousness filled with an often violent, tribal mentality to one of courage and love.

"Dare to be different," my friend Joyce Alford once encouraged a group of my friends when we were teenagers.

And the little boy born in a manger was truly different. His message to love, support and surround ourselves with others in a complex world still resonates more than two thousand years later.

There's an exciting spirit one can see in a child's eyes on Christmas morning—an abundance of energy that fills a room. Even as my Six Million Dollar Man collects dust in a closet, I still love the holiday season.

I still love the sounds of carols, a Salvation Army bell ringing and a fireplace cracklin' in the evening hours. I even enjoy the taste of a homemade fruit cake.

But it's the laughter and excitement of children that make Christmas so special. There's no doubt, as the Oak Ridge Boys sing,

The nearest thing to Heaven—is a child.

Joe (left) and brother Bill (right) on Christmas morning 1971.

A NEW STAR

Southern Spice, *Times-Georgian,* December 24, 2012

———

It was anything but a silent night.

Baby Jesus was stolen. Well, not the real Jesus, but the baby doll that played Jesus in the annual Christmas pageant at St. Margaret's Episcopal Church in 2009. This didn't happen in a rehearsal. It happened during what one longtime church member said after the service was "the best Christmas pageant ever."

My son Charlie, who was two years old at the time, made his acting debut that was worthy of receiving a Tony Award, or maybe it was more like an audition for Saturday Night Live. The pageant director Bunchie Engel cast Charlie as a sheep and his role was to crawl around the manger as the Christmas story was told.

It was improvisation at its finest. Instead of crawling around the crib, Charlie decided to crawl to the manger and take a peek at baby Jesus. That's when the trouble started.

Charlie grabbed baby Jesus and walked away with the doll tucked in his arms. Thankfully, one of the shepherds, whose job was to watch his flock, actually had to go to work. The shepherd used his crook and stopped Charlie. Baby Jesus had been rescued and "laid down his sweet head."

Once again, we listened to the Christmas story. As the storyline began to shift from the message of hope to the message of persistence, Charlie returned to the manger. I wondered if the shepherds had to work this hard at the original nativity scene? Of course, Charlie was caught again and baby Jesus returned to sleep.

As I sat in the pew laughing almost uncontrollably, I started to wonder if Bunchie somehow miscast my son. Did the Energizer Bunny appear at the original nativity? Well, he did at this Christmas pageant because for the third time Charlie returned to the manger. This time he succeeded. The shepherds put down their crooks and gave up on their mischievous little sheep.

That's when Charlie began to take off baby Jesus's clothes. I've read the Christmas story numerous times and don't recall the following line that Charlie suddenly shouted to the little girls dressed as angels.

"He's naked," Charlie told the angels as he held the unclothed baby Jesus above his head.

The little girl angels didn't quite know how to respond. I felt sorry, or more like great respect, for the narrator who continued to read the story my son refused to follow.

Furthermore, I'm pretty sure a sheep who can talk and say "he's naked" isn't in the Bible, but sometimes Episcopalians tend to twist things. So, to be sure I consulted with one of the folks at the Baptist church.

"No," answered First Baptist Minister Steve Davis. "You will not find it in the N.I.V., Living Bible or even the King James versions."

But that Christmas Eve night as the congregation held candles and sang *Silent Night*, I witnessed not only the story of the shepherds, wise men and birth of a king.

I witnessed the birth of a new star.

Author's Note: On Christmas Eve 2015, Charlie once again played an important role in the children's pageant. He played the part of Joseph where he stood next to Mary.

There were angels, animals, wise men, and shepherds at the scene. Charlie did what any good father should do. He stayed quiet and protected his son from those crazy sheep. Thankfully, no one dared to steal baby Jesus on Charlie's watch.

And everyone kept their clothes on.

Charlie stealing baby Jesus at the St. Margaret's Christmas pageant 2007.

ONE FLU OVER THE CUCKOO'S NEST

Southern Spice, *Times-Georgian,* January 5, 2014

———

The bug arrived before Santa.

It entered my house and like a row of dominos—one by one—each member of my family felt the temperature rise. And it wasn't the weather outside, but the conditions inside.

'Twas a few days before Christmas and all through my house, all of the creatures were stirring and shaking like a mouse. As our stockings were hung by the chimney with care, we hoped, if needed, a doctor would be there.

Our miserable condition stretched from our heads to our feet. And what some are calling the flu kept us off the street.

"On Advil, on Tylenol and Motrin, too," I shouted. "On Z-Pak, on Mucinex, and chicken noodle soup. From the tops of our toes to the tops of our heads, now dash away, dash away, and go somewhere else, instead."

My screaming didn't work.

I think I can safely speak for every member of my family this past Christmas won't be ranked as one of our favorites. Even my youngest son Henry, who celebrated his fourth birthday on December 25, didn't feel like eating a second piece of cake.

This will forever be remembered as the Christmas where our traditions were cast aside. All we wanted to do was survive.

For two days before Christmas, I stayed in bed. I didn't feel like reading or looking at a computer. I only wanted to sleep and watch television. And that's when I confirmed what I've known for years—I've watched way too much television in my life.

In between my naps I watched episodes of *The Andy Griffith Show, Love Boat, Gilligan's Island, The Jeffersons, Brady Bunch,* and even *The Flintstones.* I even watched part of *Days of Our Lives* and recognized some of the characters who were on the show twenty-five years ago (which was the last time I even watched an episode of a soap opera). What bothered me was not only have I seen all of these episodes at some point in my life, I knew all of the lines the characters were going to say.

It was nice to reacquaint with my old television friends for a day, but I wanted to leave my quarantined quarters by the second day. I can only watch so much television. The confinement led me to feel like I belonged in an insane asylum while my wife cared for my son Henry as he started running a fever. She tended to Henry like Florence Nightingale, but felt more like Nurse Ratched.

Despite the odds of catching this highly contagious flu bug, Santa decided to slide down our chimney anyway. Toys were delivered among the fevers, and our kids played all day. By New Year's Day, the flu bug had flown away.

It's been ten years since I experienced the flu bug. I hope it stays away for a least 110 more.

Santa is feeling OK since I know him very well. His temperature has returned to normal. As for Mrs. Claus, she's exhausted. It's tough hanging around Santa and a bunch of reindeer with the flu bug to fear. On second thought, it's not easy hanging around them every single day of the year.

So if the flu bug strikes your house, be prepared to drink lots of liquids and maybe grab a prescription of Tamiflu. Because if you don't get better, this ugly bug will make you feel like you're going cuckoo.

RESOLVING MY RESOLUTIONS

West Georgia Living, January 2014

———

I've never met a biscuit I didn't like.

So this is going to be the year to really make a change. I'm going to stick to my resolutions for 2014 to gain a few extra pounds, watch a little bit more television and cut back on exercising. I plan to fully implement the discipline it takes to succeed. It's important to have goals.

For the next few weeks, magazine covers will tempt us in the checkout aisle at the grocery store with stories ranging from "5 steps to bonding with your cat this year" to "6 things to make your hubby sexy for 2014." I'm confident I'll never bond with a cat, but I can almost assure you the writer of the sexy hubby story has never been married for longer than two years.

Since I rarely keep all of my resolutions, I've decided to implement the baseball grading system to determine my results. If I average .300 or better, then I'll consider it an excellent year. Last year, I kept many of my resolutions.

Once again, I vowed to refrain from eating any rutabagas, since they make my stomach rumble. I didn't eat one bite. I resolved to learn how to play a Billy Joel song on the piano. I learned two. I promised to spend more time sitting still, playing with my children, and taking long bicycle rides through the west Georgia countryside. Check. Check. Check. I even stuck to my resolution to never shave my chest hair despite it being the cool thing to do. Burt Reynolds would be proud.

But this year is going to be different.

I kicked off 2014 with a generous helping of black-eyed peas and collard greens while watching college football bowl games. But as for the present, the real game is on because this is the year I resolve to:

* Write the second paragraph to my novel that begins like this:

    "As Harvey washed the dishes, Delores couldn't believe her eyes. He actually was helping with household chores. She no longer cared if his T-shirt had holes. She knew this was her moment. This was her moment to surprise him with a soft kiss. Just as her heart fluttered with the excitement to embrace Harvey, he let out a large belch. Delores turned around and went back to her needlepoint. And Harvey kept washing dishes."

* Refrain from speaking any harsh language when I hear an Auburn fan shout "War Eagle."
* Refuse to utter the words "anywho," "peeps," or "we're pregnant."
* Avoid wearing skinny jeans, blue jean shorts, or any type of britches with patterns on them.
* Reconnect with old friends, create lasting memories with my family, and shell peas with old folks on a front porch.

There will be others added to the list as the year progresses, but as for now I plan to implement the discipline it takes to succeed. I'm even reconsidering eating healthier and signing up for Weight Watchers.

"I've been married to you almost fourteen years, and it's not going to be different," my wife argued. "You're the best friend a biscuit has ever had."

I refused to argue and told her I would be back soon as I pondered my future. Instead of taking a long walk, I decided to go for a drive.

With visions of a prosperous and healthier new year ahead, I knew there were other things to add to my list. So I stopped at our local fried poultry joint Big Chic to pick up a two-piece meal with fries, a dinner roll, and sweet tea.

One can't plan the future on an empty stomach.

IT MUST BE THE SALVE

Southern Spice, *Times-Georgian*, February 18, 2012

I've recently rediscovered a lifetime addiction to Vicks VapoRub. For the last two weeks I've been unable to rid this cold that makes me cough, sneeze, and breathe with what feels like a hundred pounds on my chest. Pharmacies stock volumes of cold formulas, but I've concluded that the only cure to the common cold is time.

Vicks VapoRub makes that time pass a little easier.

My grandmother, the late Inice Green of Bowdon, who I called "Maw Maw," introduced me to Vicks VapoRub when I was a child. She never used the word "VapoRub."

She referred to Vicks as "salve."

Maw Maw believed that "salve" could cure about anything. It didn't matter whether it was a cold or my muscles ached, she would always just look at me and say, "Quit complaining and put a little salve on it."

The smell of this mentholated topical cream always opened my chest, so I could breathe as easy as a Don Williams song.

Maw Maw should have been a doctor. One time when I was spending the night with her, I had a coughing attack in the middle of the night. Within seconds of hearing me, she appeared in the dark with a Mason jar full of some clear liquid and a spoon.

"Here, take this," she demanded.

"What is it?" I asked.

"It's a little recipe to help you sleep better," she replied.

The Recipe, as I called it, combined with the Vicks "salve," worked every time. I later discovered that the Recipe was corn whiskey mixed with peppermint sticks and honey.

It's still the best cough medicine I've ever sipped.

A few years ago, longtime Carroll County pharmacist Rodger Miles confirmed that Maw Maw's Recipe along with Vicks were as good if not better than a prescription.

"Just don't tell anyone," Miles said. "It's not good for my business if people convert to Maw Maw's formula."

Maw Maw's methods would eventually impact a local CEO's rise to Wall Street.

When I was in high school, I was part of the First United Methodist Church youth ski trip in Boone, North Carolina. After the first day of skiing, my friend Tee Green could hardly breathe from a bad cold.

In the middle of the night, my mother woke up Tee and applied Maw Maw's legacy of a half a jar of Vicks "salve" to his chest.

"That was the greatest medical treatment of my life," he recalled last summer almost twenty-eight years after his first encounter with Vicks VapoRub.

Last week, I watched Tee on CNBC ring the bell to open the New York Stock Exchange to celebrate his company Greenway's public stock offering. Later in the day I watched him give an interview with a reporter on the floor of this historic building on Wall Street.

As he answered the reporter's questions, he looked like a seasoned professional with crisp, clear answers. What I really noticed, however, was how good his voice sounded. It was then I realized, as he was on television in front of millions of viewers around the globe, that it must be the Vicks "salve."

Maw Maw would have been proud.

CHIM CHIM CHER-EE

Southern Spice, *Times-Georgian*, February 2, 2014

———

I decided to walk.

My wife called and asked me to join the family for an early lunch at the Highland Deli on Adamson Square. The snowfall had started and surrounded me on my short walk. Hot soup awaited and more than a spoonful of snowfall was on its way.

As the fresh scent of winter filled my senses, I recalled the words from a song in *Mary Poppins* when Dick Van Dyke's character Bert sings:

Winds in the east
mist coming in
like something is brewing
about to begin
can't put me finger
on what lies in store
but I feel what's to happen has happened before.

Within an hour, we finished our soup, and I decided to walk back to work. On my short walk, I saw a car slide into a telephone pole on Rome Street.

The snow was falling too fast. And for us folks who live in the South, Bert was right. This has happened before, but we refuse to learn and remember from our past snowy mishaps.

My 3.2 mile drive home took almost two hours. Little did I know so many friends who commuted to Atlanta would be stuck for twenty-four plus hours. Some would abandon their cars and find shelter. Others survived the cold conditions in their cars.

There's no doubt the Atlanta traffic has continued to become a nightmare. The Atlanta city streets are filled with potholes and even rush hour traffic on sunny days can take two or three hours. Thankfully, Georgia's capital city will fix the problem soon as it helps Arthur Blank and the Atlanta Falcons build another billion-dollar stadium, so Atlanta can host another Super Bowl. It's important to have priorities.

This storm was different.

First of all, the Weather Channel meteorologists even gave this winter storm a name—"Leon." Finally, after having such common storm names as Andrew, Bob, and Betsy in the past, it's refreshing to see all of those named Leon bestowed this honor. From Leon Redbone to Leon Russell, I offer my heartfelt congratulations. Even my grandfather, the late Leonas Garrett, is smiling upon us on this one.

But this storm was no laughing matter.

There were numerous children stranded and others unprepared for such an event. As I tucked myself in my warm bed on the night of Winter Storm Leon, I felt helpless as we all seemed to be in a gridlock state. I scanned Facebook pages to check on the status of so many friends stuck in this mess. In the midst of chaos and complaining, I encountered a post from my friend Laura Lenaeus, when she reprinted these words from *The Book of Common Prayer.*

"Keep watch, dear Lord with those who work, or watch, or weep this night, and give your angels charge over those who sleep," it read. "Tend the sick...give rest to the weary, bless the dying, soothe the suffering, pity the afflicted, shield the joyous; and all for your love's sake. Amen."

I wish this storm wouldn't have happened. I wish people didn't have to experience such an event. I wish Mary Poppins could have flown in from the sky and rescued so many from their distress.

In some ways she did. There were shelters, food being shared and strangers helping one another. They truly heard the words of Julie Andrews: "Come feed the little birds. Show them you care. And you'll be glad if you do…All it takes is tuppence from you."

For those of you who were stuck, I'm so sorry you had to endure this event. I hope, at the very least, you grabbed a spoonful of sugar or something stronger when you arrived home. It does, after all, "help the medicine go down."

STILL WINNERS

Southern Spice, *Times-Georgian*, March 15, 2015

―――

There's a certificate sitting in a box.

It's somewhere stored in my attic. And it probably will take a decade to find it if I start looking today. Although it no longer sits on a shelf, it doesn't bother me.

I wanted the trophy, but they were only given to those who finished first place. For a few days after my team lost, I grieved losing the title. Separated by only one point, it hurt to watch the other team receive its trophies, while all we took home was a sheet of paper. But finishing second became one of life's greatest lessons.

Recently, the Carrollton Trojans boys and girls teams competed for the basketball state title. After four quarters, both teams went toe to toe with their opponents only to fall short. The agony of defeat reminds us in sports competitions there are winners and losers when one looks at a scoreboard.

"Does it matter our boys and girls left everything on the court and were physically and emotionally spent when it was over?" said Carrollton resident and former University of Georgia tennis star Trey Carter. "Does it matter they played with character and became men and women before our very eyes? It may not matter to these boys and girls today, but it will. Anybody who has ever competed knows these things matter."

In 1997, the Carrollton Trojan football team lost a thriller in the state championship game. After the game, head coach Ben Scott told the fans and players—"We may have lost the game tonight, but there will come another time, another place—and we will win this game."

One year later, I sat in a room with Coach Scott while tears streamed down his face. Instead of quitting, the 1998 team returned to the state championship, only this time they won it.

"I never thought it would take ten years to accomplish this," he said as the final credit rolled from the season's highlight film. "We've had a plan to do this, sacrificed so many hours, and worked our tails off year-by-year to build a program to finally reach this level. We did it."

One year later, Ben died of a rare liver disease. His life and coaching career ended too soon.

Ben's legacy continues to prevail. And so does the legacy of those who came before him to pave the way for young people of today who strive to be all they can possibly be.

"It is not the critic who counts; not the man who points out how the strong man stumbles, or where the doer of deeds could have done them better," said Teddy Roosevelt. "The credit belongs to the man who is actually in the arena, whose face is marred by dust and sweat and blood... who at best knows in the end the triumph of high achievement, and who at the worst, if he fails, at least fails while daring greatly, so that his place shall never be with those cold and timid souls who neither know victory nor defeat."

One day these young men and women will look back with a different set of eyes. They'll still feel the jabs and pain of losing the state title on a cold, rainy night in Macon, Georgia. But this time, there'll be no tears. They'll look back with a smile.

I should know. There's a certificate still lost in my attic to remind me.

THE LONG GOOD-BYE

Southern Spice, *Times-Georgian*, April 22, 2012

———

It wasn't supposed to be this way.

There were supposed to be cookies made for her grandchildren. There were supposed to be games played with them. There were supposed to be many things grandmothers simply do.

"Dad, what's wrong with Gran?" inquired my seven-year-old son Will.

"She has a disease called Alzheimer's," I replied. "As you know, some people have heart problems, cancer and other ailments. Gran has a disease that takes away her memory and the ability to do things that she did so easily for years."

"Is there anything I can do?" asked Will.

"Unfortunately, her disease will not get any better," I answered. "All we can do is just give her extra love and lots of hugs."

"OK," Will replied. "I can do that."

I don't know exactly when it started. In hindsight, I can point to the time my keys disappeared in her clothes drawer while visiting. I can point to the time she seemed to draw a blank on someone's name, but then again—who doesn't do that every now and then?

"Even the highest trained physicians can't recognize Alzheimer's in the very early stages," said Dr. James Lah, associate professor of neurology, Emory University School of Medicine, and a physician in practice with Emory Healthcare.

The signs started to really point towards an issue when my mother started repeating the same things over and over again. I wanted to deny this was one of the first signs of someone with Alzheimer's. I wanted to sweep it under the rug and move on with life as usual.

I wanted to say she's fine.

According the Alzheimer's Association, there are 5.4 million Americans with the disease. Between 2000 to 2008, the proportion of deaths due to heart disease, stroke, and prostate cancer decreased by 13, 20, and 8 percent, respectively, whereas the proportion due to Alzheimer's increased by 66 percent and is now the sixth leading cause of death in the United States.

It's a disease some people are still embarrassed to talk about.

"Back in the old days, we thought people were going crazy," said my ninety-year old great aunt Sara Harman. "No one wanted to talk about it."

The old days, however, aren't that old.

The turning point of removing the negative stigma and embarrassment from the disease came in 1994 when Ronald Reagan wrote a letter to the American people revealing his diagnosis of Alzheimer's.

"Upon learning this news, Nancy and I had to decide whether as private citizens we would keep this a private matter or whether we would make this news known in a public way," Reagan wrote. "In the past, Nancy suffered from breast cancer and I had my cancer surgeries. We found through our open disclosures we were able to raise public awareness. We were happy that as a result many more people underwent testing. They were treated in early stages and were able to return to normal, healthy lives.

"So now, we feel it is important to share it with you," Reagan continued. "In opening our hearts, we hope this might promote greater awareness of this condition. Perhaps it will encourage a clearer understanding of the individuals and families who are affected by it."

On Easter Sunday, my mother had an accident where she broke her humerus bones in both shoulders that required two surgeries in three days. While my mother was in the hospital, I would sit with her for a few hours not really talking much.

For several stretches of time, we sat there in silence.

It was then I realized what real prayer is to me. It's not about asking for a miracle or asking to even make things easier.

It's about being together even if nothing is being said.

STILL WALKING

Southern Spice, *Times-Georgian,* September 22, 2013

———

I t's no longer about words.
Although we still communicate, our conversations have evolved to small talk. As my mother's mind continues to succumb to the mental tidal wave known as Alzheimer's, another season has evolved in this journey many call "the long good-bye."

There is nothing anyone can do. There is no medical cure at this time. There is no hope we will return to the days of my mother walking into a room and raising the energy level, as people would erupt in laughter from her contagious spirit.

Despite the difficult path and a fairly certain future of the degenerative stages ahead, she's still here, and so are an estimated 5.4 million people in the United States living with this disease. There's a story in every neighborhood that will break your heart.

"My mom lived with Alzheimer's for about seven or eight years," said my friend Dr. Buck Miller. "It is, what I would call, a regressive rather than progressive disease. I believed it was my duty to embrace it and see it as an act of God's wisdom, so I did. I took comfort in being able to be guidance, be the teacher, be the 'adult' to her 'child.'"

And it's not only the 5.4 million people afflicted with the disease who suffer. Although you won't find it in the *Diagnostic and Statistical Manual of Mental Disorders*, the people who provide care suffer from an unofficial disease called "Caregiver Syndrome."

According to Wikipedia, an estimated sixty-six million Americans are caregivers to a chronically ill loved dependent. And 70 percent of those caregivers suffer from depression.

As the conversations now have become very brief with my mother Betty, I noticed our communication is mostly a hug and a smile. In some ways, I see her as a newborn baby who mirrors a parent's smile before the baby has the ability to speak.

"Is it not true, that each of us see beauty in the naiveté, the innocence of a child?" said Dr. Buck. "So to others I would suggest seeing the disease as an opportunity for one's loved one to relive the wonderment of childhood, and for us to embrace the blessing of being afforded a chance to 'give back.'"

Life can take away our promises, our memories, our hopes, and our dreams. It can punch us so hard in the gut we may feel we can never stand again. It can take away all of these things and so much more.

Even though my mother's mind continues to move away, it's OK. The disease may take all of these things. But no matter how long she lives or what her future circumstances may be, Alzheimer's can't take away my mother's spirit and the love she's shared with so many through the years.

And it damn sure can't take away her soul.

SILENT MEMORIES

Southern Spice, *Times-Georgian*, October 5, 2014

———

The pound cake was still warm.

It wasn't the first time. For most of my life, she never hesitated to cut a few slices and walk across the street to deliver. Sometimes she would even invite the neighborhood kids inside her front door to devour a piece or two.

I'm not sure who was happier. As much as I loved biting into one of Jean Muse's hot pound cakes, I think she was happier than anyone else. Besides, her health often prevented her from eating sweets, but it didn't prevent her from raising our spirits with an overdose of butter and sugar.

For forty-plus years, Jean and Newt Muse lived in the same neighborhood as my parents. And the Muses moved four times. Three of those times the Garretts and Muses lived across the street from each other, but never on the same side (it's important to have distance).

Both Jean and my mother raised a household of boys. It's probably extremely safe to say each one of us drove them crazy from time to time, but they never hesitated to put us in our place.

"I'll never forget when we were all young teenagers, your momma lectured me, you, and your brother Bill one day and said, 'Boys if you don't want any trouble in life—chew bubble gum, drink Coca-Cola, and keep them britches zipped up,'" said Jean's youngest son, Donnie. "That's how I learned about the birds and bees."

It's a wonder Donnie remembered that lesson. He's only got five children. And he's an ordained music minister, too.

As Forrest Gump once said, "Momma always had a way of explaining things so we could understand."

Ten months before Jean died, Donnie and I loaded up our mothers and treated them to lunch at Billy Bob's Barbecue. Here we were, years removed from our childhood, only this time the roles were reversed. There was a time when you couldn't get a word in the conversation, but on this day half of the group was silent.

Both my mom and Jean were in an advanced stage of Alzheimer's.

One of the toughest parts of watching two women who were once full of life and energy was simply watching them. They sat across from each other and didn't speak. They communicated with smiles and occasionally even laughed. Donnie and I told old stories hoping there was connection inside their brains somewhere.

There are no instruction manuals for these situations. However, there are ways to communicate. Expecting those suffering from memory loss to always reply in conversation is about like expecting your dog to ask, "How's your day going?"

It's usually best to refrain from asking them questions and to talk to them. They seem to enjoy that. And even though they're silent doesn't mean they don't enjoy the sounds of young children's voices and a beautiful choir. They're still here. And so are you.

It's hell watching someone go through the stages of memory loss. There are no words to describe it unless you've been there. Medical researchers and the rest of us don't have a solution or cure for this terrible disease. This I know and so do you.

But somewhere there's a thin place. It's not between us and them. It's a connection, and the walls are very thin. We're all on the same team and want this disease to cease. And that reminds me there's something bigger than life's complexities.

There's got to be a little bit of heaven in this somewhere.

*Joe (left), brothers Bob (middle) and Bill (right) with
their mom Betty and dog Champ 1976.*

SEARCHING FOR MEANING

Southern Spice, *Times-Georgian*, November 3, 2013

―――

The scars never leave.

As Horace Jeter's troop walked through the jungle to reach the base of Black Virgin Mountain in Vietnam in 1969, the intense awaiting of another battle loomed. It would not be the first time his troop faced combat. For some members of his troop, however, it would be their last.

"It was very scary, and we didn't know what to expect," said Jeter. "We lost eight men in that battle, forty were wounded, and one man was missing in action."

It was one of many battles Jeter faced after his appointment to the infantry. Once he entered the field, his life would never be the same.

"I didn't sleep much because we usually fought at night," said Jeter. "There were many nights where I sat in the middle of the jungle in pouring down rain back-to-back with a member of my troop keeping watch. We were restless, hungry, and so delirious. It was either do or die. We called it hell."

Throughout those nights, Jeter dreamed of returning home to his family in Carrollton. He hoped to return to his love of playing drums in his band. He prayed that he would reunite with his classmates from the 1967 class of Carver High School.

"Every male in my senior class with the exception of one was drafted in 1968," said Jeter. "Our class would never be complete again because our classmate Larry Graves lost his life in the war."

Jeter almost didn't return when his troop was ambushed, and he was wounded by shrapnel. His body was hit in four places and barely an inch above his eyes. He has the scars to prove it.

"My friend Smitty pulled me away from the battle after I was struck and saved my life," said Jeter. "After I was wounded, I returned home. Smitty saved my life and to this day we still talk on the telephone once per month."

His return home was another war.

"I remember being spit on and called 'baby killer' by people at Hartsfield Airport when I arrived in Atlanta," said Jeter. "It was extremely difficult adjusting to civilian life. I was sick from Agent Orange and the shrapnel wounds. I had enormous guilt from the battles where we killed the enemy from gunfire. I prayed to God daily for forgiveness."

Jeter also entered one-on-one counseling following the war.

"My counselor encouraged me to not go through life always dwelling on the past," said Jeter. "He encouraged me talk about it. And I do. I continue to this day to seek support from my classmates who still get together regularly and others members of my troop who fought with me in Vietnam."

But Jeter's scars and memories of war are a never-ending battle.

"I still wake up with nightmares," said Jeter. "And it's been forty-four years. I was a teenager when I entered the war and did my job. However, I still question the war. I question why killing people is the way to solve problems. I question it all.

"I will always continue to seek counseling and surround myself with others for support," said Jeter. "I even occasionally speak to school groups. Young people today play so many violent video games for fun. I know that's part of being a kid, but there's nothing fun or glamorous about war."

The Vietnam War divided our country in so many ways. Those who served didn't return in ticker tape parades or accolades.

"Within two months of returning, I went to work," said Jeter. "You don't feel good about war. But despite the pain, the guilt, and the agony I felt, I knew I had to move on. And I did."

Every day is still a struggle for Jeter and thousands of others who recall horrific scenes from combat. No words that can take away the pain of those who served. However, we all have the capability to tell our veterans the most important two words in the dictionary.

All we have to say is "THANK YOU."

EASY TO LOVE

Southern Spice, *Times-Georgian*, November 4, 2012

———

Our hearts are hurting.

My family and I can't quit crying, and we feel like we're walking through hell while our friends are lifting us into heaven. The loss of a child has been described as the hardest thing in the world, and last Saturday night we became a member of a club no one wants to belong when our precious eight-year-old son Will was tragically killed in an accident at Adamson Square in downtown Carrollton.

This wasn't supposed to happen, but it did. We've lost our sweet boy, and we can't get him back. Our tears flow and somehow, someway my family has to move forward. And we will.

During the last few days, my family and I've felt the hugs, love, and prayers from an overwhelming community. Even from those of you who we've never met who've sent messages and prayers. May God bless you all. You've all helped us beyond words. All we want to do is put our arms around this community and beyond to say "thank you, thank you, thank you."

I can't imagine my life without Will. He always smiled. As a baby, I always called him my "smiling child" because of his contagious grin that could light any room. I'm going to miss our bicycle rides around the college. I'm going to miss taking him to his school at Oak Mountain Academy. And even our days when I skipped work so he and I could go ride a roller coaster at Six Flags or climb Stone Mountain.

I'm going to miss watching him playing outside. Whether he was collecting insects or butterflies, digging our yard, playing with sticks, jumping on the trampoline, and so much more that little boys love to do, I can't help but know he lived his life never wasting a minute.

I'm going to miss him making our coffee. How many kids do you know that grind beans and make coffee for their parents? Or, even fry or scramble an egg for breakfast? He loved these things. He even asked for a leaf blower for his birthday which he used almost daily to keep our driveway clean from pine straw and leaves.

But it was music that he loved the most. Two weeks ago, he entertained the students at Carrollton Elementary School when he played drums alongside his favorite teacher Terry Lowry and me in our little band we created for the school's annual Fairy Tale Ball.

He formed a special friendship with his uncle, David Stark, from Houma, Louisiana, who taught Will how to hit the drums so our neighborhood could hear him from miles away. I broke down when David, who alongside his brother Joe recently finished recording with the same producer who's worked with Bruce Springsteen, Pearl Jam, and Paul McCartney, said they plan to dedicate their first CD to Will when it's released nationwide next year.

His piano skills were amazing, as he loved playing everything from Beethoven to Warren Zevon's "Werewolves in London." He loved an audience and never hesitated to play when a piano was near.

"He loved to play 'Fur Elise' which is supposed to be played slowly, but he played it fast and upbeat," said Lowry. "One day I said, 'Will, do you know what's behind this song? Beethoven had just broken up with his girlfriend and he was heartbroken.'"

"You mean he didn't have to have a girlfriend any longer?" Will replied. "Cool."

"And of course, he turned 'Fur Elise' into a happy song," Lowry said. "That was so awesome."

There's no question now why my family chose to make Carrollton our home. It's this wonderful community who is surrounding us when we need it most. As we sat around friends this past week, my priest Hazel Glover remarked, "It looks like a slice of heaven in this room."

All we can say to each of you is "We love you." You have lifted me and my family when we've needed it most. And because of that we can reach to the sky and feel the touch from something so much more.

We can feel the touch from our little angel.

Will Garrett 2008

A SEASON TO MOURN

Southern Spice, *Times-Georgian,* December 2, 2012

A t times, the pain is almost unbearable.

It doesn't go away and when it strikes, there's not enough football gear in the world that can shelter me from these intensive hits.

I see him everywhere I go. Even when I pump gasoline into my car, I can see him peering through the window. When I drive the kids to school, I see the empty seat. When I hear a song on the radio he loved, I see him turn red from embarrassment when I would catch him singing.

I used to go to work refreshed and ready to start the day. These days I cry alone in my car for several minutes before I can even walk through my office door.

Everything looks different now. I want to talk football with friends. I want to celebrate the holiday season, which is normally my favorite time of year. I want to smile and feel normal again. I want all of this and so much more—but I can't. All I want for Christmas is to bring back my eight-year-old son Will, and not even Santa Claus can do this.

"It has been said the death of a parent is the loss of one's past," writes Ronald Greer in his book *Markings on the Windowsill.* "The death of a spouse is the loss of one's present, and the death of a child is the loss of one's future."

I've only visited his grave a few times. Last week I went alone with his classical guitar that he was learning to play. As I played a song I looked for a sign, but there was none. I wanted to see an eagle flying above, like I did after his graveside service. I wanted to find another butterfly, like the one my mother-in-law found on the spot we decided to bury him.

"Just wait," said my friend Beverly Kaiser who lost her daughter Jill fifteen years ago to cancer. "There will be many more signs to come, and his presence will be felt all around you."

Trivial things absolutely drive me crazy right now. When I read posts on Facebook about bad service at a restaurant or someone's dissatisfaction with political leaders, I want to shout at these people and remind them for just one second how lucky they are.

In 1965, the music group the Byrds released a single, based on the passage from Ecclesiastes, when they sang "To everything there is a season." If this is true, then I'm walking through the intense season for mourning. But I'm not alone.

We all go through this season. Of course, some go through more seasons than others. Some experience pain more than others. But we all, if we live long enough, will walk through this season of grief.

The late Jim Callahan once remarked that "all go on and that the shores on which we stand are closer than we think." My love for Will Garrett is so vast I can't imagine it being anything else but eternal. I can't explain it. I can only embrace it.

So, as I start another day, I can't make the pain go away. All I can do is hear the words Pete Seeger wrote and recorded by the Byrds. All I can do is "turn, turn, turn."

Will (right) and Turner (left) at Wrigley Field in Chicago 2011.

SWIMMING UPSTREAM

Southern Spice, *Times-Georgian,* January 27, 2013

————

T ime keeps ticking.

There's a world going on even when I want it to take a break. I'm going through the motions of my daily routine like always, but everything looks different. The overwhelming feeling of grief continues to drive my family's life.

We're hurting. The pain hasn't eased one bit since the night my eight-year-old son Will died three months ago. I cry until my stomach aches. All I know is since my son went to Heaven, his absence has left my life fractured.

I want him back. I want to tuck him into bed and sing a song to him before he falls asleep. I want to go out in the yard and watch him ride his bicycle again. Oh, how I miss him.

As I read the newspapers every day, tragedy is all around us. Even this past week, the students at Central High School in Carrollton, Georgia, are mourning the loss of their seventeen-year-old classmate who was killed in a car accident. We want to ask "why?"

There are no answers. There are no words.

My friend Steve Davis wrote a wonderful column in November 2012, titled "Reflections on what not to say." In his column he shared the words from a family who had lost an eleven-year-old son. After spending the last three months as a parent who has lost a child, I find this story worth repeating.

"Please don't ask if we are over it yet. We'll never be over it. Please don't tell us he is in a better place. He isn't here with us. Don't say that at least he isn't suffering. We haven't understood why he had to suffer at all. Please, please don't tell us you know how we feel, unless you have lost a child. Don't ask us if we feel better. Bereavement isn't an illness that clears up. Please don't tell us that at least we had him for eleven years. What year would you choose for your child to die? Please don't tell us that God never gives us more than we can bear. We don't believe God gave us this tragedy. Just say that you are sorry. Please just say that you remember him. Just let us talk about him. Please just let us cry."

So, how do we walk further with someone suffering through an almost unbearable feeling of grief? My honest answer is "I still don't know," but here are some of my reflections since becoming a parent who has lost a child.

Please don't be afraid to mention the deceased's name. I used to be afraid to do this for fear it may cause the bereaving person harm when he or she needs just the opposite. I believe most people long to hear their loved one's name called once again. If one begins to cry, it's OK. It's another tear to help a person heal.

Often times, we want to provide comforting words and try to fix or take away someone's pain. In times of enormous grief, words are always said with the best intentions, but I must confess that hugs are better.

So instead of trying to lift those or hurry them out of the ditch, jump in with them. As Dr. Ron Greer writes in his book *Markings on the Windowsill*, "What is needed is support, closeness, understanding—not cheerleading. What is needed is someone caring enough to visit, courageous enough to ask how the heartbroken person is feeling and wise enough to be quiet and listen."

Oh, how my heart aches for the family of the student who was killed this week and the Central High School student body. The road ahead is going to be so difficult because there are no shortcuts through grief. I've got to believe there are still bright days ahead. I've got to believe somehow, someway we'll fully engage an abundant life again and find the inspiration to be all we can be.

I only wish it was going to be sooner.

ONE LESS SET OF FOOTSTEPS

Southern Spice, *Times-Georgian*, March 24, 2013

———

He's not there.

After searching for sunny skies for most of this winter, I'm longing for warmer temperatures in the southern air, hopefully soon. I'm ready to watch my children outside again. Whether they're members of a make-believe army fighting aliens or pretending to fly a rocket ship to the moon, it warms my heart to watch kids just be...well, kids. I try to find a smile, but I struggle as a tear rolls across my cheek.

There's one missing.

After losing my eight-year-old son, Will, last October, I start to think about my expectancy to live another forty years with this pain...this emptiness...this longing to be with Will again. Everyday feels like I have "one foot in eternity and the other on shaky ground," as I once heard in a Rick Tarquinio song.

"It's been eleven years since I lost my daughter," a friend of mine recently told me. "Do you know what I still do every single morning? I cry my eyes out and then I get dressed and go to work. Then I do it again before I fall asleep. It is what it is."

I walked by Will's classroom recently as his former classmates prepared to leave on a field trip to the Georgia State Capitol. It was the same trip I promised him I would chaperone at the beginning of the school year. The parents and students were excited. All I could do was walk quickly to my car so no one would see my tears.

We had too many plans. We had too many bike rides, Six Flags trips, places to travel, music to make, and the list never ends. But the plans are gone. They're all gone.

I hear stories of parents upset with their child's coach, as if being moved from second base to right field is a disaster. There are many things in life so much more important.

I won't ever watch Will fall down, make mistakes, and pick himself up again. There will be no graduations, wedding, children, and all of the joys of hanging out with him.

This is against nature. This isn't the way life is supposed to be.

Then I turn my eyes to my other three children playing in the yard. I see their smiling faces, hear their laughter, and I find joy, hope, and a promise for the future in them. I see Will in each of them, and I know that his zest for life lives on in them and in their spirits.

The pain of losing him will never abate, nor will the gaping void of his absence ever diminish, but loving my living children gives me happiness in this new world where happiness seems hard to find most of the time.

Recently, my six-year-old neighbor Lilee-Raye Cousins walked over to my house while I was working outside. She asked me if I'd ever heard the song "This Is Not the End."

"I played it for Will after my grandmother died," she said. "Will really liked this song."

I used the power of technology and downloaded the song on my iPhone, and we listened.

"This is not the end…This is not our last breath…We will shine like the stars bright, brighter," the song says.

"I think of Will when I listen to it," she said while the song was playing.

And then I heard another lyric from the song—"And you know you'll be all right."

It was as if she'd sent me a message from Will. Maybe we are going to "be all right." I looked at her and said, "Thank you. Every time I listen to this song, I'll think of Will, too."

Once again, I looked to the sky. Once again, my memories flooded for my precious son. Once again, another teardrop began to fall.

The Garrett boys (L-R) Charlie, Will, Turner and Henry 2011

MOVING FORWARD

Southern Spice, *Times-Georgian,* May 26, 2013

Babe Ruth no longer lives here. Neither does Sinatra, but the city that never sleeps still lures millions of people per day to this giant slab of concrete called Manhattan. Once again, I returned to the Big Apple to experience a fast-paced world 928 miles away from my daily life in Carroll County.

Usually, I'm here for business, but this trip was for fun and a Tom Petty concert.

I toured the city with a couple of native New Yorkers, along with another friend. These Yankee friends knew how to navigate the busy streets and subways, along with picking the perfect spot for a hot dog, coffee, and a bagel.

We toured the East Side, the West Side, Upper, Lower, and everything in between to embrace a world far away from the Little Tallapoosa.

This trip marked my first excursion to Yankee Stadium only to be denied entrance due to a rainout that was supposed to pit former Cy Young Award winners C. C. Sabathia against R. A. Dickey in a pitcher's duel. So, instead of seeing the newest version of the "house that Ruth built," we walked two blocks in the Bronx to see the apartment building where Ruth lived, across the park where Al Pacino chased the bad guys in the 1970s classic movie *Serpico.*

"You know what I love about this city," said my friend Howard Seeman, as we walked through Central Park. "Unlike Carrollton where you know everyone's business, you see a person on the street and have no idea how he got to New York. He may be incredibly successful, a survivor of 9/11, or even a Broadway star. Everyone has a story."

Many of these American stories started at Ellis Island. This area of 27.5 acres became the gateway for immigrants arriving past the Statue of Liberty to begin a new life.

Our country is one with deep scars, as others arrived against their will in chains and shackles on slave ships. Even though America still promotes opportunity, liberty, freedom, and justice for all at its core, it's not perfect. But it's still the land I want to call home.

Despite our differences, religious, and political beliefs, I saw evidence of how America charges forward.

As we slowly rode through Ground Zero, all I had to do was look to the adjacent block to see the spiraling unfinished Freedom Tower rising among the scaffolds and cranes to eventually become the tallest tower in our land.

"My brother was walking to work near the World Trade Center when he looked above his head and saw the airplane make the turn towards the twin towers," said Seeman. "His sons, who were in a nearby school, watched people jumping out of the windows. It changed us all."

The tragedy of 9/11 continues to haunt our fragile world. As I looked at the new Freedom Tower under construction, I was reminded how lucky I am to live in a country that may be knocked down from time to time, but always manages to rise up.

It's always fun to travel to the Northeast. A New Yorker's life is fast-paced, crowded, and full of energy. And for forty-eight hours, I was a guest in this metropolis.

On my last day, I felt like I had walked a marathon in a hurried pace when a group of street musicians stopped me in my tracks. It was near the Bethesda Fountain featuring the neoclassical sculpture, also known as "Angel of the Waters," in Central Park.

For two minutes, I listened to the most beautiful rendition of "Amazing Grace" I've ever heard.

Seven months ago, I probably would have kept walking. But this time I stopped, and I began to cry.

For the first time in my life, I really didn't care if anyone was watching.

OUR TOWN

Southern Spice, *Times-Georgian*, October 20, 2013

I had the city to myself.

In the early morning hours of October 26, 2012, I decided to explore Carrollton by pavement as I jogged in darkness while the rest of the world slept. With the exception of a few cars passing me on Maple Street, the slight autumn breeze in the air kept me company.

Businesses were closed as I made my way to Adamson Square, and for a few minutes I was the only person in this historic part of town. In just another hour, the hustle and bustle of people driving to work and school would fill the streets. But for this brief moment everything was quiet with the exception of my shoes squeaking on the sidewalk.

I could have chosen another place to live—perhaps a city with an ocean view, tall skyscraper, or a place where the mosquitos don't bite. But this is my home.

I love walking into a restaurant, a grocery store, and almost anywhere else and seeing people I know. I love my short commute of less than fifteen minutes to work on a bad traffic day. I love the tall pine trees, the blooming azaleas along Dixie Street in the springtime, the small lakes for catching brim and catfish, and the farmlands with rows of corn, beans, and okra.

I love living in a community with manicured ball fields, beautiful golf courses, paved roads to ride my bicycle along rolling hills in the countryside, and the soon-to-be completed GreenBelt that will be the largest paved loop trail system in the state of Georgia.

I love living in a college town showcasing one of the prettiest landscaped campuses in the country at the University of West Georgia. I love a town that embraces the arts, music, and good food. But most of all—I love this town because it's a wonderful place to raise a family.

By no means do I suggest Carrollton, Georgia, is perfect. It has its obstacles like any town in America. Some of these things are beyond control, but others are not.

Adamson Square in the center of town has for more than a century served as the hub of Carrollton for businesses and entertainment. In the last fifteen years, the square has evolved from a struggling economic climate to become a picturesque atmosphere filled with restaurants, shops, and bars. It's only a matter of time before Hollywood discovers its beauty, charm, and setting to showcase all that's good about the South.

With the recent addition of an amphitheater, Adamson Square has become even more of a thriving hub for food and entertainment. But it's missing something. Despite its charm, it's missing the most important ingredient to be the ultimate showcase.

It's not safe for pedestrians.

Unfortunately, it's taken the death of my eight-year-old son Will to highlight this flaw in our traffic system. Hopefully, our leaders can make a difference.

In the next few days, I want to invite everyone to visit the Square, cater to the restaurants and shops, but most of all—take time to stand on the sidewalks and observe the crosswalk signals.

They are flawed.

When the pedestrian signals give you permission to cross, the traffic lights also give cars turning left or right the right of way to keep driving. In other words, cars and pedestrians are given the "green" or "go ahead" lights at the same time.

I'm not an engineer or even an expert in traffic safety. However, pedestrian safety can be improved.

It's pretty simple. When a pedestrian light gives the clear to cross the crosswalk, a car shouldn't be given the light to turn right or left. It takes only fifteen to twenty seconds to cross a crosswalk. Why can't traffic stop for a few seconds and allow pedestrians to cross? Why can't we give pedestrians some peace of mind? Why can't we hopefully save another life?

The City of Carrollton has started taking the necessary steps to update the pedestrian signals and make changes, but it's not enough yet. Hopefully more steps will continue to be taken.

On the night of October 27, 2012, the last words I said to Will were "Let's go. We've got the light." The truck hadn't turned yet. We had the crosswalk signal. The driver had the green light.

And my family had to bury my son a few days later.

AUTHOR'S NOTE: In 2014, City of Carrollton officials eventually changed the traffic system through Adamson Square. All stop lights now go red when pedestrians are crossing the street.

I HURT MYSELF TODAY

Southern Spice, *Times-Georgian*, October 27, 2013

——

The accident changed him.

When he was twelve years old, J. R. decided to go fishing. His fourteen-year-old brother, Jack, took another route and went to work. He told J. R. the family needed the three dollars he could earn by cutting trees into fence posts.

The boys' mother didn't want either one to leave the house because she noticed Jack seemed different that day.

"What's wrong?" she asked, before they left the house.

Jack said he didn't feel right and thought something was going to happen. Both J. R. and his mother begged Jack to stay home, but he left anyway. J. R. walked with him hoping he would change his mind.

A few hours later, J. R. returned from the fishing hole when his father and his preacher drove up in a Ford Model A to tell him that Jack had been in an accident. He had cut himself on a table saw.

A week after the accident, Jack took a turn for the worse and told his family members at his bedside the end was near.

"Can you hear the angels?" he asked his mother. "They are beautiful. It's a beautiful place where I'm going."

J. R. never got over his brother's death. For the first twelve years of J. R.'s life, his brother was always by his side. J. R. wanted to be just like him. He looked up to him. He admired him.

Jack was his best friend.

J. R.'s journey was filled with pitfalls and shortcomings. When he began to work his way through drug addiction, he credited his brother's spirit for bringing him through.

There's a powerful bond between children and their parents. But never underestimate the bond between two brothers.

J. R. later described his grief as "creating a big, cold, sad place in my heart and soul." He said whenever he was in a dark place, he would sing the songs from Jack's funeral and it would "give me peace, and I can feel God's grace flowing."

The world would go on to know J. R. as Johnny Cash. Even until his dying days, Jack was more than a brother. He protected Johnny in death, as he did in life.

On this day last year, I had a strange feeling when I arrived at the soccer fields to watch my ten-year-old son Turner's game. After Turner exited the car to join his teammates, I noticed my eight-year-old son Will had yet to eat his lunch in the car.

"What's wrong?" I asked. "Do you feel OK?"

"Yes," he said with a melancholy voice. "I don't really feel like eating right now."

A few minutes later, Will walked to the edge of the woods next to the soccer field.

Something appeared different.

Instead of running around like always, he was sitting under a tree, as if he was meditating.

That memory still gives me chills.

I wish we would have stayed home that night. I wish we would have ordered a pizza delivery and helped my wife, Ali, and sons Charlie and Henry carve the pumpkin.

After picking up the pizza, Turner and I watched the most horrifying event no one should ever have to witness. Within seconds, he helped me pull Will from underneath a truck and begged his brother not to die.

For eight and a half years, Turner and Will were inseparable. Born twenty-one months apart, they played together. They laughed together.

They shared a room together. Turner never had a chance to say good-bye to his best friend.

None of us did.

In the years ahead, I'm sure Turner will choose his own course. I'm sure it will be quite different from Johnny Cash. I'm sure he will face many obstacles and challenging moments. But like Johnny in the toughest of times, Turner will always have his brother.

And through the pain, tears, and darkest of days, I know like Turner—the rest of our family will have him, too.

Will (left) and Turner (right) in their last picture together 2012.

Turner (left) and Will (right) in Seagrove Beach, Florida 2012.

Turner (left) and Will (right) at Sanford Stadium in Athens, Georgia 2012.

*Turner (left) and Will (right) on the bank of the Chattahoochee
River in Whitesburg, Georgia 2011.*

SPRING

———

Suppression brings depression. Expression brings resurrection.

—Ronald J. Greer

DANCING IN THE WIND

West Georgia Living, May 2014

———

Here, outside my backdoor, somewhere along the walk to grab the morning newspaper, it hits me.

As the sun peeks through the pine trees in my front yard, I feel a difference...a change...almost as if something's coming. Can't really explain it, but mixed among the cool air is a touch of warmth. It's a touch of something I haven't felt in long time, but I recognize immediately.

Easter is celebrated this time of year, along with sounds of lawn mowers on ball fields and crickets chirping throughout the night. The tulips in my neighbor's yard return once again to remind me life goes on. And so it does.

As I walk into my garage, I notice my bicycle needs recharging by pumping air into the tires. Within minutes, I climb aboard its uncomfortable saddle and leave my driveway. For a few seconds, I'm eight-years-old again.

Only this time, I have no clear destination. Just to ride with a slight breeze in the crisp air and return home in a couple of hours, that's all I have to worry about—at least for the moment.

My journey starts along the rolling hills throughout Carroll County. With names like Salem Church, Buttercup, Victory, and Farmers High—I have the countryside to myself along with some cows, a few barking dogs, and a fox I spot several yards away. West Georgia is a cycling paradise. Perhaps it's our best kept secret with the beauty, charm, and peacefulness of the sounds of spinning wheels and an occasional cranking of a John Deere tractor from a nearby farm.

Eventually, a car passes and I'm reminded of what's good in this world. Instead of throwing something at me or shouting ugly words for slowing the driver down, people in this neck of the woods do what Southerners do best—they wave at me, a total stranger who has come for a visit.

The day awaits back home when I return. There will be moments of household chores and watching the kids play around the house. I hope to spend some time today encouraging my son to take the training wheels off of his bicycle so he can learn the freedom and joy of riding a bike. For a moment, there'll be no iPads, iPhones, computers, or Xbox games. Only a boy and his bicycle—the freedom of doing nothing (even if for a little while).

But here I am—alone and on the road. Do I go straight? Turn left? Or right? And then I know. I decide to keep heading towards Shiloh Church and eventually turn right along Davenport Road, past the old arbor that's served for more than a hundred years as a hub for camp meetings and revivals.

Once again, I arrive at the cemetery and the spot of my son Will's burial. He would be ten years old this May. I stop for a moment and look at the ground, as a river of tears flows from my eyes...the pain of loss... the thoughts of what will never be...the longing just to hold him one more time. After a few minutes, it's time to leave.

Here I am, once again, on the road returning to life and a home. My legs are tired, but my heart wants to move on. As I turn left on a new road, I see wildflowers sprouting alongside a pasture fence with a butterfly dancing in the breeze. Why here? Why now?

And then I can't help but ask the big question. Life goes on, doesn't it?

The real answer is I truly don't know, but for this moment—I believe it does. That's the promise of springtime.

I can feel it in the air.

IF YOU BELIEVE

Southern Spice, *Times-Georgian*, March 27, 2016

———

Yes, Henry, there is an Easter Bunny.

And she's hippity, hoppity, as she moves along her way. Maybe she's back home and relaxing after an all-night journey of delivering Easter baskets to all of the little girls and boys.

In the next few years, you'll have more friends who will no longer believe in the Easter Bunny. It's highly likely you'll follow in their footsteps as you begin to question a bigger world. But it doesn't have to be that way.

When I was a six-year-old boy just like you, I remember waking Easter morning to find an Iron Man action figure and a stuffed rabbit next to my bed along with some chocolate candy.

I believed in the Easter Bunny then. And I do now.

Henry, I've never seen the Easter Bunny, and, now that I think about it, I've never seen the Tooth Fairy either. But that doesn't mean they don't exist.

Yesterday as I took a walk among the pollen in the air, I felt a slight breeze against my face. And then it hit me. I've never actually seen the wind. Sure, I've felt it my entire life and even on occasion watched its mighty power after storms. And like the Easter Bunny, I know it's there.

Easter is celebrated across the world by millions of people. Through the next several years you'll hear stories of Jesus. You'll hear various opinions of the man who radically changed the world. Always listen with an open mind, but more importantly, please take the time to read the stories yourself.

We live in a broken world where religion is often at the core of division. Henry, I believe your soul is on a journey and whatever path you choose, may you always choose love.

Don't ever think you're not worthy. You are.

Always keep your ego in check, but know life is about something bigger because as the old saying goes, "Playing small doesn't serve the world." Furthermore, remember "EGO" stands for "Edging God Out."

As you grow older, you'll begin to realize many adults view Jesus as a grown-up version of the Easter Bunny. That is, if you behave, do great things and ask for things that are often self-serving—then the Easter Bunny will always do nice things for you.

Unfortunately, life doesn't always work that way.

The Easter experience for our family will always be viewed through a different lens. A few years ago, I stood inside St. Peter's Basilica at the Vatican. Inside this magnificent cathedral in Italy, there is a stunning statue carved by Michelangelo called the "Pieta." The statue depicts a grieving Mary holding her son Jesus across her lap shortly after his death.

It's hard for me to view this Michelangelo masterpiece because it mirrors too closely how your mom and I held your brother after his accident. It's a powerful work of art. And I will always feel a deeper level of connection to Mary and any parent who has lost a child on Good Friday.

Life is hard. Life is difficult—and extremely complex.

The Jesus story describes a man who challenged us to love unconditionally—to expand our consciousness that every person may have life, dignity, abundance (even your enemies)—and to be all we can possibly be. Most importantly, there's the promise of Easter—the promise of a better day ahead. The promise life goes on.

Henry, do I believe in the Easter Bunny? I believe in all things that come from a source of love. And I can promise you on this Easter morning as you and your brothers eat chocolate eggs from your baskets—the Easter Bunny came with more love than you can possibly imagine.

Joe and Henry in Ft. Lauderdale, Florida 2013

LIBERTY FASHION

Southern Spice, *Times-Georgian*, January 11, 2015

———

They buried him in his Liberty overalls.

For ninety-five years, Raymond Hughes wore them better than anyone else. A lifelong lover of the outdoors, he was at home when he rode his tractor, grabbed a fishing pole, or took a ride in his 1971 Chevrolet Short Stepside blue and white pickup truck to run errands in town.

And in the summertime, there wasn't a better friend. My guess is he shared the wealth of his tomatoes, cucumbers, and squash with half the residents of his hometown.

"They don't make them like him anymore," I overheard someone say while standing outside the funeral home.

And through it all—the war, the work of raising two daughters and later caring for his late wife of sixty-five years who suffered from dementia, Raymond kept moving ahead.

And he did it wearing his overalls.

"I wonder if Raymond's death wasn't just the end of a good man?" said my friend David Hughes. "I wonder if Raymond's death might have signaled the death of the overalls? You just don't see many old men wearing them anymore."

Perhaps it's true.

My grandfather Robert Green wore them almost around the clock. His Liberty overalls were rugged and patched in the knees from tilling his garden with an old mule and plow.

"Men who wear overalls don't have a lazy bone in their bodies," said David. "I can't always say I trust a man wearing a suit. But, by golly, I've never met a dishonest man wearing a pair of Libertys."

Well, maybe so, but I must confess there's at least one pair of Libertys a person should question—the Hee Haw overalls.

"Oh yea, I had a pair of yellow ones," said David. "I used to pretend I was picking a banjo like Stringbean or telling jokes like Junior Samples every time I wore them."

In the 1970s, Liberty produced a vintage assortment of overalls with the donkey logo from the long-running television show *Hee Haw* which aired for twenty-eight consecutive years on Saturday nights, from 1969 to 1997.

"Just like I had to go to church every Sunday, my grandmother used to make me sit and watch *Hee Haw* every Saturday night," said David. "That wasn't so bad. The worst part was I had to watch *The Lawrence Welk Show* after *Hee Haw*. Now that was torture.

"But I loved my Hee Haw overalls," continued David. "I once dated a girl and told her about how I used to wear them. She broke up with me after that, and it's probably for the best. Last I heard about her is she got drunk one night and hit her ex-husband over the head with a can of Campbell's chicken noodle soup. Just think, if it wasn't for Hee Haw overalls, I might have married that girl."

But Raymond Hughes was a class act in his faded blue Libertys. And the fellow who said, "They don't make them like him anymore" hit the right note. They don't.

These salt-of-the-earth, homespun men, who served our country and members of the so-called Greatest Generation, are leaving us in large numbers. And so are overalls.

Thank God some network recently started airing repeats of *Hee Haw*. At least there's a glimpse of sunshine in all of this somewhere.

Robert "Paw Paw" Green with Joe (left) and Bill Green (right) 1973

AGE OF TRUTH

Southern Spice, *Times-Georgian*, August 30, 2015

———

I'm stuck in the middle.

It's not that I don't enjoy the friendships with people my own age. I do, but I connect better with children—and old women.

Somewhere on the ends of each spectrum I'm pulled towards these groups of people. On second thought, I'm actually drawn towards these folks, not pulled.

It's where I feel most at home.

"That's completely normal," said local psychology expert Matt Carter. "People your own age usually tiptoe around your emotions out of respect. Old women and children tell you the truth."

I decided to test the local expert's insight, and it didn't take long to realize his brilliance when I ran into my friend Ms. Delores in the produce aisle at Publix.

"Well, I read your column in yesterday's newspaper," said my friend.

"That's great," I told her. "I appreciate you taking the time to read it."

"As a matter of fact, we talked about it at the beauty shop this morning," she continued. "We all agreed it wasn't nearly as good as your column from two weeks ago."

I started laughing.

"I'm not joking," she said.

Once again, I smiled and hugged my friend.

"I hope you like the one that'll be in this Sunday's newspaper," I said.

"Oh, I'll let you know," she said, as I walked away.

A couple of hours later, I again tested the theory when my eight-year-old son, Charlie, jumped into my lap a few minutes before bedtime. He started tapping on my stomach.

"Dad, your belly sounds like a watermelon," said Charlie. "You've got a big belly. I think you eat too much."

He was right. I hugged him and tucked him into bed. As I walked out of his room, I suddenly had a craving for a Snickers bar and a glass of wine.

Maybe the songwriter Tom T. Hall had it all wrong. Instead of old dogs, I believe it's old women who "care about you even when you make mistakes."

And I totally agree with him when he sings "God bless the children while they're still too young to hate."

Because when I focus on the things that really matter, I realize there ain't but three things that's worth a dime. And that's old women, children, and watermelon wine.

TRUCKING FOR JESUS

Southern Spice, *Times-Georgian*, May 19, 2013

―――

I t's the end of the world, and I didn't even know it. And I feel fine. Last week I drove my dad to a doctor's appointment in Atlanta. While sitting in the waiting room, I began to browse through the seven-year-old copies of *Sports Illustrated* when the news was delivered. Instead of hearing it on CNN, I heard the breaking headline from one of the patients waiting for his name to be called.

The man was wearing a trucker's cap and an orange airbrushed T-shirt both with the single word "Jesus" printed on them, as he sat down next to another and spoke his prophetic words.

"The end of times is near," he said to the person sitting next to him.

As the man continued to share the gloomy news about our planet, I began to hope I could make it to the Varsity for one last chili dog lunch before the world ended.

What if he's right? What if the end is near?

But then I couldn't take my eyes off his trucker's cap. I couldn't get the song "Give me oil in my Ford and keep me truckin' for the Lord" out of my head. I could tell the stranger sitting next to him was impatient and ready to return to the waiting room's 1992 April edition of *Better Homes and Gardens*.

That's when he caught me staring at him. All I could do was smile. Thankfully, he looked away and continued talking to his new friend about the end of the world. Once again, I began to ponder if he's right. What if the end is near?

I've always thought I would be sitting in a waiting room when the world ends, and I have proof. It's the old eighty/twenty rule that's taught in business schools with a little twist. In other words, I've spent 80 percent of my waking hours waiting while I've actually been living the other 20 percent. It's as if my life was destined to stand in lines and be placed in rows.

Perhaps Dr. Seuss said it best. In his book, *Oh the Places You'll Go,* he writes about the "waiting place."

> *"Waiting for a train to go*
> *or a bus to come, or a plane to go*
> *or the mail to come, or the rain to go*
> *or the phone to ring, or the snow to snow*
> *or waiting around for a Yes or No*
> *or waiting for their hair to grow.*
> *Everyone is just waiting."*

Like Dr. Seuss's words, we are all waiting. Some of us are waiting to watch our gardens grow while others are waiting in line to ride a roller coaster. Some of us are waiting in line to pick up kids from school while others are waiting on lab results that could change one's life.

Do good things really come to someone who waits? I would argue yes–sometimes.

"It all comes down to a choice," said Tim Robbins' character in the movie *Shawshank Redemption.* "Get busy living or get busy dying."

As another week begins, I hope to make the most of the present moment and leave the worrying to the fellow with the trucker's cap. He seemed to have all of the answers while I continue to live in a world of questions.

I hope he's wrong, and the world isn't coming to an end. I hope he can find life worth living while the sun's still shining.

Most of all, I hope he can find joy in his life—even if it involves wearing an airbrushed T-shirt.

COMMUNITY NEWS

Southern Spice, *Times-Georgian*, March 6, 2016

———

I 've a feeling we're not reading about Kansas anymore.

We're not even flying somewhere over the rainbow. No longer does one travel by dirt road to reach Kansas either. All one has to do is leave Adamson Square in Carrollton, pass through Burwell and eventually hang a left on Melear Road to reach the community.

Kansas is situated a few miles from Buncombe and within walking distance on a blacktop road to the community of Jake. If one is ever lost, there's no need to panic because all roads lead to Mt. Zion.

I miss the days of reading about these tiny spots of local dwellers. For years, the community news of Shady Grove, New Hope, Roopville Route One, Abilene, and others dominated the pages of my local hometown newspaper the *Times-Georgian*.

Writers such as Mrs. Winnie Baxter, Sara Tuggle, Mary Garrett and other locals updated the community before the Internet and Facebook made it a daily occurrence.

For people who have moved to the Southeast within the last fifteen years, they may think they've arrived in the land of Oz if they should ever read one of these clippings from the archives. For those of us who remember these weekly reports, however, I long to read them once again.

Like Dorothy, last night I had a vivid dream. Instead of traveling to the Yellow Brick Road, I became the gossip columnist and chief reporter for my small fictional community. After spending a week visiting with family, friends, and church members, I recorded all the local events to submit for publishing. The following is my report:

Chapel Heights Route 9
by Mr. Joe Garrett

We had a wonderful day at the early morning church service, with almost a full house, including several visitors.

The men's quartet sang "Church in the Wildwood" and "Dropkick me Jesus through the Goal Posts of Life" and did a great job.

After the morning services, fruit baskets were taken to the shut-ins. Please continue to pray for Mrs. Jones and her nephew Hoyt. Mrs. Jones had a stomach bug last week, while Hoyt has a bad case of the gout.

Happy Anniversary to Snuff and Sheila on March 9 and Brother Davis and his wife Lucille on March 11. Both couples plan to celebrate their special days by taking a drive to Rome to eat at the Golden Corral. Snuff's brother Gerald, who is a Godly man, plans to join the couples by driving from his home in Rossville.

Last week, the members of the Agape Sunday School class hosted a soup-and-sandwich lunch to benefit the youth group's mission trip to Tennessee in June. There were lots of side dishes and desserts, including Mrs. Morrow's fried pies. We enjoyed the fellowship.

Rev. Roscoe Taylor and his youngest daughter Wylene are spending several days with their relatives here. Sunday they attended church.

Several members of the 1943 Centralhatchee graduating class met at the home of Mr. and Mrs. Johnson on Saturday night for a grill out. They ate hamburgers, hot dogs, and some special fresh sausage from Mrs. Johnson's nephew who slaughtered a hog named Ramona last week. A good time was had by all.

Also, continue to remember our prayer list: Mrs. Mozelle who's battling an in-grown toenail; Mr. Staples who cut part of his finger while working on his lawn mower; Ms. Cindy who's suffering from bursitis; and Coach Criswell who tripped over a chicken while playing basketball in his grandmother's yard last weekend.

My sincere wish to each of you is a happy and healthy week ahead.
May each of you be blessed with all that is good.

We may never see classic journalism like the small community reports again. None of these columnists won a Pulitzer Prize for their weekly writings, but they informed their readers of big events.

How else would we have known about Hoyt having a "bad case of the gout?"

SUNDAY MORNING COMING DOWN

Southern Spice, *Times-Georgian,* March 9, 2014

———

A Sunday morning drive in the rain kept my mind on the road as I listened to a screaming preacher on AM radio.

I'm not sure what channel or even the whereabouts of the fiery voice, but I'm quite sure if I wasn't "washed in the blood" by the time I reached Trickum Valley, Alabama, then trouble awaited me before I escaped Cleburne County.

The list of all my sins was long as Brother Jonas shouted at me through the airwaves.

"I don't know—uh—a where you're a going, but I know—uh—where I'm a going," Brother Jonas shouted in his fast talking voice. "They is all kinds of sinning—uh—going on. They is all kinds of lusting—uh—going on. But they is only one thing—uh—that's gonna get you through..."

Suddenly, my mind began to recall too many shortcomings. I thought about everything from that time I bit Joe Murrah in his front yard to hiding the *Sports Illustrated* swimsuit issue with a half-naked Kathy Ireland on the cover in my underwear drawer.

Joe Murrah eventually bit me back and my mother found the magazine. So, in order to save my soul, I shouted back to Brother Jonas "I repent," in case I got pulled over for a traffic citation when I reached Ranburne.

I often try to picture what these screaming preachers on Sunday morning AM dials in the South look like.

My guess is most of them are "sweaters." Even when the temperature is below thirty degrees, they perspire. And I have a strong feeling most of them like a good all-you-can-eat Sunday buffet. A man needs to eat after burning a thousand calories while screaming at sinners.

Maw Maw was a big fan of screaming preachers. Any time I visited her on Sundays, she always had her radio dialed to an AM gospel channel.

"Maw Maw, that man sounds like he's about to get into a fight," I said.

"Oh no, he's just telling it like it is," Maw Maw replied.

She would then return to making a batch of homemade biscuits, and I would continue to listen to the radio preacher wondering if he was about to suffer a heart attack.

Although the occasional shouting pastor can still be heard across AM dials on Sunday morning throughout the Bible Belt, I often wonder for how much longer?

The world of religion and church attendance is forever changing. According to the Pew Research Center, the fastest growing church in America isn't the Catholics, Protestants, or Evangelicals. It is what I once heard someone refer to as the "Church Alumni Association." Even the screaming, sweating AM radio pastors are disappearing.

The reasons for this decline point to personal priorities getting in the way. In this fast moving, electronically connected world, folks are living busy lifestyles from catching up on work to the new trend of children playing organized sports on Sundays, hoping they will become one of the less than 1 percent who ever makes it to the professional ranks.

However, the biggest reason for the shift according to Pew Research points to an issue directly related to religion or the church itself. Those reasons are manifold in a world of "I'm right" and "you're wrong" mentalities.

All I know is on a dreary, wet Sunday while driving through the rolling hills of Alabama, Brother Jonas shouted through the airwaves for us to take time to "be good to your friends—uh—love your brothers and sisters—uh—be kind to your coworkers—uh—and please take time—uh—to go visit your momma."

As Brother Jonas finished his message, a choir sang a version of "Just a Little Talk with Jesus" slightly off key. I sang along and felt a little brighter. And then I thought of Maw Maw and how much she would have enjoyed Brother Jonas.

His message would have uplifted her and we would have heeded to his commands to "repent"—at least for the next few hours.

And that my friends—uh—is telling it like it is.

WHAT'S YOUR HURRY?

Southern Spice, *Times-Georgian,* October 13, 2013

———

I t wasn't the Sermon on the Mount.

However, it was delivered a few miles from Mt. Pilot when Dr. Harrison Everett Breen delivered a sermon to the members of the All Souls Church in the fictional town of Mayberry.

The local folks wanted to look their Sunday best for the visitor because he wasn't just any traveling preacher. He was "from New York" and his sermon topic was "What's your hurry?"

"As I stood there during the singing of the hymn, I asked myself, 'What good message can I bring to the good people of Mayberry?'" Dr. Breen said. "Everything today is run, run, run. We drive ourselves from morning to night. We have forgotten the meaning of the word 'relaxation.' So I say to you my friends—relax, slow down, take it easy."

Barney and Gomer fell asleep during the message, and the rest of the community might as well have. The words missed the congregation, as they spent the rest of the day doing the exact opposite.

"My husband and I were talking about everyone being so busy the other day," said my friend Nancy Hall. "No one wants to sit on a porch and do nothing anymore."

We no longer spend our Sunday afternoons sitting on the front porch like my great aunt Lizzie used to do. And I don't blame television, video games, or iPads for the death of front porch sitting. I blame society for no longer making it acceptable for the women of the family to dip snuff.

I never saw Aunt Lizzie get bored or ever complain she had nothing to do. However, I did see her hiss at one of my cousins when he tried to steal her old Maxwell House coffee can she used for a spittoon. Aunt Lizzie found her joy on the front porch.

It's hard to sit still. Even if it's for only ten minutes without any noise, doing nothing can often be viewed as a sign of weakness—but perhaps it may be the source of all strength.

"Stillness is where all creative endeavor is born," said best-selling author Eckhart Tolle in his book *A New Earth*. "So it's getting in touch with the stillness within, where there's no mental noise, and out of that stillness, when the time is right, sometimes an impulse comes. Something—a feeling, a strong sense that something wants to be born into this world."

Recently, I spent a weekend afternoon sitting in a folding chair as my children played outside. I left my telephone, iPad, and books in the house and observed.

The white clouds hovered above my head surrounded by a blue sky. Some leaves began to fall as indication another season is on the horizon. And I heard laughter from children around my house.

There were no thoughts of yesterday. There were no worries about tomorrow. All that really mattered was the present moment of watching life evolve in all of its majesty.

"There's nothing easy about this journey we're all on, is there?" my friend Hazel Glover looked me in the eyes and asked me this past week.

"No," I quickly answered.

Maybe it was Dr. Harrison Everett Breen who said it, but I think it's the words attributed to Jesus when we're faced with pressures, worries and the storms of life. In moments when we feel like we're walking upstream, he didn't say "be more judging," "be ready to fight," or "be more religious."

He simply said, "Be still."

BARE IN THE WOODS

Southern Spice, *Times-Georgian,* February 10, 2013

———

Blame it on professional wrestling.

A couple of years ago to my wife's dismay, I introduced my two oldest sons Turner and Will to the fine sport of professional wrestling. As a man who has reached middle age, I can now reflect on the impact of watching *Georgia Championship Wrestling* on Channel 17 during my childhood.

What is the impact? I can still pin my brother Bill in a full nelson, should he ever decide to attack.

We haven't wrestled on the floor of my parents' house in almost thirty years, but you never know when a wrestling move may come in handy. Should Alabama ever decide to invade Georgia, I think I may be able pull out some of my old wrestling techniques in defense. I may even decide to wear a cape and mask so those invaders from Alabama know I mean business.

As for my children, it didn't take long to realize the impact professional wrestling was making in their lives. One day when I arrived home from work, I discovered them on their trampoline stripped down to their "tighty whitey" underdrawers wrestling each other.

"Look at what you've started," said my wife Ali. "I don't like them watching wrestling."

I tried to explain since I grew up in a family with all boys that our sons' decision to strip in the yard and wrestle was quite normal, but I don't think I succeeded. Then again, I'm not sure what constitutes as "normal" anymore.

Since we buried my son Will at the Shiloh United Methodist Church Cemetery last November, I've noticed a sign posted to a tree where a walking trail connects to the graveyard. Last week, my father-in-law, Randy Turner, read the sign and suggested I do the same thing.

NOTICE. THIS IS PRIVATE PROPERTY, I viewed while clearly understanding the intentions of the sign. "Protected by invasion of privacy law…You are welcome to use these grounds to walk, jog and etc. by permission. Please keep pets on leash."

At this point, I was ready to move on. However, I decided to study the sign in its entirety. I'm glad I did.

"No offence is inended to anyone," I read noticing the sign's incorrect spelling. "These grounds are used by nudist at times."

I scratched my eyes and reread the last sentence again.

The cemetery has been my place for refuge, tears, and meditation since Will's passing. On this day, my mind began to shift from grief to ask myself, "How do I greet a nudist should one appear in the woods next to the graveyard?"

I decided to seek counsel from a member of the clergy.

"Instead of asking the nudist to put his clothes back on, start a conversation," said my childhood friend Rev. Gil McGinnis, pastor of the First United Methodist Church in West Point, Georgia. "Just say something like 'Sure is nippy out here today, isn't it?' or 'Your face sure is familiar, and it's only your face I'm looking at. Do you have relatives buried here?'"

As I continue to return to this cemetery and adjust to my "new normal," I promise to be ready should I encounter a naked man walking in Burwell, Georgia.

Since my grandmother Thelma Garrett is also buried in this peaceful place, I promise to show her my respect. I'll do this in the absolute best way I know how—I'll keep my clothes on at the cemetery.

She would be proud of me.

MADE WITH LOVE

Southern Spice, *Times-Georgian*, February 24, 2013

———

A biscuit has always been there.

However, for the next forty days and forty nights, I've decided to give up something during Lent that's a lifelong staple in my life—biscuits. When it comes to my lifelong addiction to hot, buttered biscuits, I've been what my Aunt Edith has described as "spoiled rotten."

My mother always made homemade biscuits from scratch. Within minutes of grabbing the White Lily flour and Crisco from her kitchen cabinets, my mother could "whip up" a batch of biscuits faster than most people can put a store-bought canned biscuit on a pan.

When I first asked my mother how she made biscuits, she didn't say the words flour, a bowl or buttermilk.

"I make them with love," she replied.

And she did. For almost forty years, she made a pan of biscuits almost every single morning. I never heard her complain. My brothers and I always had friends spend the night on the weekends and we never had to extend an invitation.

They invited themselves because they knew my mother would cook them biscuits.

Thankfully, biscuits continue to serve as a staple on the southern breakfast table. Almost every fast food restaurant cooks them, but I'm partial to our locally owned establishments who still make them from scratch. My mother believed canned biscuits weren't real biscuits.

"If you can read, you can cook," my mother always preached to us.

The problem with her advice is she never wrote down her recipe. Furthermore, how do you teach someone to master cooking a fluffy biscuit when the true skill can't be expressed in words? My mother's biscuit dough was more of a craft than art. On second thought, maybe it was more art than craft. Either way, it's tough to duplicate my mother's biscuits.

Biscuits even played an important role in my destiny. Most people who relocate to the South are surprised to learn we can take salmon out of a can, bread it, and fry it.

After my wife Ali and I started dating, her mother Lynde Turner invited us to dinner. I couldn't believe my eyes when I realized we were having salmon paired with biscuits, English peas, and mashed potatoes.

I wanted to ask her mother if I could propose to her daughter after my first bite, but I decided to see what other things her mother paired with biscuits for future meals before asking for her daughter's hand in marriage. Furthermore, it didn't take long after eating my wife Ali's biscuits paired with sausage, bacon, country ham, roast beef, cubed steak, and fried chicken I realized there was something divine occurring.

I'm thankful for biscuits.

They have helped me start my mornings and have sometimes even soothed my evenings for years. Within twelve hours after my son Will was killed last October, I heard a knock on our door, as the sun peeked through the clouds. My friend Valerie Ayers appeared at the door with homemade biscuits.

A hot, buttered biscuit was the first thing I ate after the tragedy. Even in the midst of the most horrific time of my life, a biscuit brought me comfort.

After I learned the skill of making biscuits, I quit making them a few years later because I could never make them taste like my mother's. Alzheimer's has now robbed her ability to prepare the things she once performed daily without ever looking at a recipe.

Maybe I need to try once again to cook my mother's biscuits. I probably should go see her sister and perfect my skill. Hopefully, if Aunt Edith succeeds in teaching me—I plan to make a hot pan of these divine delicacies. And then I'm going to make a trip.

I'm going to take one to Momma.

SHOWING UP

Southern Spice, *Times-Georgian,* January 31, 2016

———

O n a rainy winter afternoon, I reached to turn off my ignition switch.

In the rearview mirror, I glanced at the people entering the backdoor at Almon Funeral Home. It was a somber occasion as I prepared to open the car door to pay my respects. As my feet touched the damp pavement, I realized my journey was complete.

"There will be another day when you have the courage to go inside," a voice in my head said. "You've come far enough today."

I've attended a few funerals and visitations since losing my son, but I've missed so many. Thank God other people surrounded these families when I couldn't even muster the strength to walk inside and recall the nightmare of standing next to a casket.

Great literature, music, and poetry have often haunted me when dealing with death.

Jay Gatsby knew how to throw lavish parties for hundreds of people in F. Scott Fitzgerald's *The Great Gatsby*, but when he died—only a handful of people showed for his funeral.

Furthermore, Willy Loman's life, in Arthur Miller's play *Death of a Salesman*, ends tragically, as none of his friends, customers, and colleagues pay their respects.

Even the lyrics of the Beatles classic song "Eleanor Rigby" describe the lonely life of an elderly woman who dies alone.

Eleanor Rigby, died in the church
And was buried along with her name
Nobody came

One night a few years ago, I answered a phone call informing me of a tragic death of someone close to my wife's family. When I told my wife, she immediately started shaking.

"I don't know what to do or what to say," she said.

And then she remembered the advice her grandmother gave her years ago.

"You go," instructed her grandmother, who lost her son in a car accident in 1973. "You go and sit with the family right now."

That's exactly what my wife did.

Three years later, my family would find our lives on the other side of tragedy.

"The pain I have now is the happiness I had before," wrote C. S. Lewis. "That's the deal."

I vaguely remember who was there in the most dreadful moment of my life after losing my son, but my family felt the presence of so many. Words cannot express our gratitude in such a dark time.

At one point while sitting in a room at the hospital shattered, shocked and feeling a sense of hopelessness—I do, however, vividly recall four people who sat with us. Two of those had lost a child and the other two had persevered through tragic situations of their own.

These friends knew exactly what one should do when tragedy strikes close.

They showed up. They said nothing. They cried with my family.

And most of all—their presence carried us.

GOOD-BYE YELLOW BRICK ROAD

Southern Spice, *Times-Georgian*, August 25, 2013

———

T hey say California is the place you want to be. So I loaded up my SUV, drove to the airport and flew south of Beverly. Hills that is, swimming pools, but I didn't see any movie stars.

California is a world apart from Georgia. I truly understand why Jed and Elly May Clampett, Granny and Jethro Bodine picked southern California after Jed struck oil shooting at some food. The mild weather is perfect year-round with a slight breeze always in the air.

As I write this column, I'm overlooking the Pacific Ocean. I'm also wondering if this may be the only sunshine I'll see for the rest of the year due to the monsoon Georgia summer. I don't want this weather to go away, but to paraphrase the late singer-songwriter and San Diego resident Jim Croce, "Oh, I've got to get out of here...because California's not my home."

That's why I'll once again return to the land of the Little Tallapoosa.

For three days, I've become a tourist exploring this beautiful city, sandwiched between the Laguna Mountains and the blue waters of the Pacific.

My first night I watched a jazz band at a bar owned and managed by Jim Croce's widow. Although the music was really good, something seemed out of touch since the jazz band played Tony Bennett instead of "Bad, Bad Leroy Brown."

Since I arrived in this beautiful city I've eaten fish tacos, taken long early morning walks along the marina, and watched a Padres baseball game. But the highlight of my trip is right now sitting on a beach listening to the ocean waves crash in front of the Hotel Del Coronado.

This is the same hotel featured in the 1959 Oscar winning movie *Some Like It Hot* that teamed Tony Curtis and Jack Lemmon with Marilyn Monroe. Throughout the hotel are artifacts about the movie along with all of the pictures of famous movie stars and dignitaries who've graced this hotel, from Ronald Reagan and John Wayne to Frank Sinatra.

I've often longed for a scarecrow and a yellow brick road in my life, and as I relax outside this historic place—I realize Emerald City is closer than I think.

For it is here L. Frank Baum wrote three of his *Wizard of Oz* books. He lived in the Hotel Del Coronado off and on for several winter seasons and even designed the stately chandeliers that still hang in the hotel.

Some historians believe the scene in the movie when the Scarecrow chops down the chandelier in the witch's castle and the lights go out only to be relit moments later is a tribute to Baum's writing ability for finding light within his dark stories.

"Those who do not find Coronado a paradise have doubtless brought with them the same conditions that would render heaven unpleasant to them did they chance to gain admittance," Baum said in a 1904 newspaper interview.

Here I sit with my toes in the sand as the sunset falls over the horizon.

I hear laughter from the folks sitting at a nearby bar. I can see surfers trying to catch the next wave. I can even hear a guitar player singing "Fire and Rain" in the distance as the aroma of fresh-cooked seafood lingers in the air.

And yet here I am in the midst of a California dreamlike atmosphere with teardrops falling from my eyes as I long to click the heels of my flip flops three times and fly over the rainbow to see my son Will.

It's been almost ten months since we lost him. As I close my eyes, I realize I've got to keep searching for light in the darkness of grief. Though I long to always travel and see beautiful places, I understand how Dorothy felt.

I miss my family and am ready to return to the place I love the most. Even while I sit in paradise with an ocean breeze in my face, I realize there's something better.

Because there's no place like home.

TYING MY SHOES

Southern Spice, *Times-Georgian,* December 29, 2013

———

T ime, oh good time, where did you go?

Another year has passed. Another 365 days have eclipsed our lives. And it feels like it's rained for at least 298 of those days. It's been a wet year.

For many people, their lives have been enriched with fortune and success. For others, they've experienced pain, hardship, and suffering. As for me, I'm somewhere in the middle as I've been surrounded by love and good health even though I'm still plowing through the deepest grief since losing my son Will in 2012.

Death changes you. It takes you to a depth of pain that at times paralyzes your thoughts, words, and actions. Everything becomes an accomplishment including tying your own shoes and walking out the door.

"I think I'm losing it," I said to my friend who lost a child several years ago in a tragic accident. "I can be laughing one minute and within seconds the tears flow like a stream. I live with a horrific scene that never stops playing in my head from watching my own child die in my arms."

"You're not losing it," he said. "Let me diagnose your situation.—It's called grief."

"I don't know what to do," I continued. "I get up every morning, get dressed, take my kids to school, and go to work. I'm able to function, but I feel like I've aged fifty years. I want this bad dream to go away. I don't know what to do."

"Keep moving," he said. "Just keep moving forward through this deep valley of grief."

And I have.

Even in the midst of darkness, I'm finding glimpses of light. I'm even finding days where I'm truly enjoying life again. It's not a destination. It's living at a deeper level. It goes way beyond bumper sticker religion.

People often suggest for me to put my faith in the heavens above, but it hasn't been easy. I try to pray, but often I can't find the strength. I try to picture my son in a better place, but I want him back home enjoying the holidays with his family and playing with his brothers.

Part of this is selfishness on my part, but I can't help it. I want him back. I want to ride bikes with him, watch him play outside and tuck him into bed at night.

I'm sure there's a magic pill I could swallow that may numb this grief and pain for a little while. But I've got to feel these emotions. I've got to feel the depths of this enormous sorrow. Because to feel these emotions is to feel the boundless love I have for my son.

"Grief has a way of showing you just how deep your aliveness goes," writes Alison Nappi in her column titled "5 lies you were told about grief." "If you allow yourself the chance to feel it for as long as you need to—even if it is for the rest of your life—you will be guided by it."

In the next few weeks, we'll all forget our new year's resolutions. That's just part of living. But there's one resolution I know I've got to do. Even if 2014 brings many days of rain, I know what I've got to keep doing. And so do you.

It's really simple when you think about it. It's just two things. Grab a raincoat and most of all—keep moving.

BIG EASY LIVING

Southern Spice, *Times-Georgian*, March 30, 2014

———

T he dialect is like no other in the world.

Within minutes of hopping in my cab from the Louis Armstrong International Airport, I knew where I was when the driver said, "I hope you're ready to eat."

The late CBS News Correspondent Charles Kuralt once wrote, "Unless you're broke or sick or blue-nosed, I don't see how you can't have anything but a good time in New Orleans."

A business conference brought me to the Big Easy, but my primary mission was simply three things: food, friends, and good music—and in no particular order.

On the first morning, my feet hit the pavement of Canal Street, as the sun was rising. Among the street cleaners, joggers, and beggars, I walked toward the levee banks of the Mississippi River to begin my day with beignets and café au lait at the Café du Monde. I've tried to make this chicory-filled coffee at my home, but it never tastes the same as sitting in this classic establishment opened in 1862.

"Most of us were settled by Anglo Saxons and Puritan types," said Joe Cahn in Kuralt's book *America*. "The work ethic prevailed and all the pleasures of life were frowned on. It's real simple. Work ethic equals bland food.

"We were settled by Catholics from Spain and France who thought work should never interfere with the enjoyment of life," continued Cahn.

"And that's what makes this place different from the rest of America. People in New Orleans believe in living in the present, skimming off as much pleasure as they can today and eating as well as they can tonight. That goes for everybody. If you go to confession and say to the priest, 'I overate, Father,' you'll probably have his interest right away. He'll probably ask you, 'Where did you eat?'"

For the next three days my palate consisted of spicy grilled oysters, po' boys, andouille sausage, gumbo, boiled crawfish, and shrimp. Jeremy Davenport and his jazz band kept me entertained at the Davenport Lounge. The former trumpeter for Harry Connick, Jr., filled the room just a block away from Bourbon Street with New Orleans sounds each evening.

But the best of all occurred fifty-seven miles south of the Crescent City. After my class ended, my friend Keith Weisheit drove me south to Houma to visit with friends. We filled our bellies with Cajun cooking and capped off the night dancing and playing music at a local dive.

The great theologian John Wesley once wrote, "When you catch on fire with enthusiasm, people will come for miles to watch you burn."

Perhaps Wesley was hanging around a bunch of future Louisiana settlers when he said this.

It's been said "Nothing good happens past midnight," but this night was different. My friends Billy Stark, Kyle Domangue, Michael Klaus, and I jammed with the Voodoo Bayou Band until we closed the joint at 2:00 a.m., with me singing lead vocals on the John Anderson song "Chicken Truck."

Within forty-eight hours, Billy would be back in his law firm, Kyle would be drawing architectural plans, and Michael would be teaching music to children in a local school. As for me, my ears would still be ringing.

Seventeen months ago, Billy and Kyle played musical roles in my son Will's funeral. On this night, these guys reminded me life is to be lived. And it's better with food, music, and great friends. It's not only good for your life. It's good for your soul.

Laissez les bons temps rouler!

TURNING POINT

Southern Spice, *Times-Georgian,* July 6, 2014

———

W e craved pasta.
Among an evening with a light mist of rain outside, my family walked across the street from our hotel to Ristorante Paoletti, a cozy little restaurant on Main Street in Highlands, North Carolina.

While we waited for our server, I surveyed the room for families with small children. There were none.

Most parents cross their fingers when they take their young children to a nice restaurant. As for my wife and me, we order a bottle of wine. It's no longer about romance. It's about sanity.

Within seconds of sitting at our seats, the server arrived with menus. The choices would be difficult whether to order the Risotto al Limone ai Frutti di Mare, Scampi con Broccolini o Fra Diavolo, or Involtine di Pollo alla Boscaiola. In other words, did I want shrimp, scallops, or chicken?

I felt like I was in a Dean Martin song.

Highlands is a tiny little town with a total area of 6.2 square miles located on a plateau in the Southern Appalachian Mountains with a population of 924. It's elevation at 4,118 feet contributes to its mild temperatures in the summer months.

We've been coming here for several years and enjoy the short drive through the small towns before crossing the Miller J. Grist Bridge to climb the mountain to Highlands.

There's a small church on almost every block. Shops close early here. And the pace is slow.

Highlands is really a place to come relax and sit still. Some may call it doing nothing and boring. I call it therapy.

My children enjoy it, too—the candy store, the toy store, the coffee shop. It never seems to change. But I miss the old Cyrano's Bookshop on Main Street, the little store filled with novels, biographies, and regional books. It closed a few years ago as another casualty to the Kindles and easy online reading sources available today.

In 2009, I encountered best-selling author Pat Conroy on the street behind the old bookstore while strolling my sons Turner and Will. For a few minutes, time seemed to suspend as this celebrity author of *The Lords of Discipline, The Prince of Tides,* and *The Great Santini* visited with us. We talked briefly about our mutual friends Shea (Jackson) St. John and Joe Cumming from Carrollton before he signed a copy of his latest book *South of Broad* for my children.

The little things of breathing mountain air or staring at a stream or waterfall make time spent here enjoyable, but I'm a sucker for the little boutique restaurants.

As the desserts arrived to our table, the laughter escalated. While we devoured bread pudding, lemon sorbet, chocolate gelato, and tiramisu, I realized the birth order theory in full swing as my four-year-old Henry became the comedian. And he didn't have any wine.

Henry talked about body parts and everything else you can imagine most people consider impolite dinner conversations. Although we tried to curtail his words, we realized "a wild boar sometimes can't be contained." So instead of exploding over the way Henry was giggling, we decided to join him. And so did a few tables around us.

Sometimes it takes a child to lead the way.

When the bill arrived, I almost had a heart attack. While my family walked out of the restaurant, I stopped by the restroom. Once inside, a few tears trickled down my face. My family was laughing in the midst of carrying the heaviest burden of grief. Only this time, I cried tears with a smile.

As I walked toward the exit of the restaurant, I thanked the hostess for a wonderful meal and excellent service. I did, however, keep a secret from her.

I would have gladly paid more.

The last Garrett family photo made two weeks before Will's death.
(L-R) Turner, Will, Ali, Charlie, Joe and Henry.

TWO YEARS

Southern Spice, *Times-Georgian,* October 26, 2014

———

T he train whistle echoed as the conductor shouted, "All aboard." A young woman outstretched her hand to help her grandfather climb the steps, while his wife screamed for him to "hurry up," as she sipped a Diet Pepsi in her seat.

He made it. And within a few seconds, the sounds of "clickety-clack, clickety-clack" filled the warm air on this August day as the train left the station.

"Maybe we should catch the train on the way back," I said to my son Will, as we unloaded from our car at the base of Stone Mountain.

Within a few days, Will would be starting his four-year-old kindergarten class, perfecting his coloring skills, and putting together his ABCs. But on August 29, 2008, he was smiling from ear-to-ear as we walked. Although the climb is a relatively short hike, in his mind we were climbing Mt. Everest.

He was never in a hurry.

Will jumped on every rock and our journey took a little longer than normal. Old men and women, who I suspect once had little children of their own, stopped to speak to him. For a few seconds, his contagious spirit touched them, as only as a child can do.

"Dad, have you ever climbed Stone Mountain?" Will asked.

"Oh sure, several times since I was your age," I replied. "My mother even said she made this same walk when I was in her tummy."

As we approached the summit, we decided to sit and gaze at the sky-line of Atlanta. We didn't say anything to each other. Sometimes peace and sitting still are God's greatest gifts.

Later that night, I hugged and kissed Will and his brothers as I tucked them into bed. When I exited their rooms, I remember think-ing, "It doesn't get any better than this."

That day with my son was a glimpse of Heaven. There were no streets of gold or crystal rivers—only a four-year-old son and his dad spending time together. Someone else can dream of the golden roads. My dream is to see my son again.

Tomorrow marks two years since my family lost him.

I wish I could tell you it gets better. It doesn't. I wish I could tell you the pain has slowly subsided. It hasn't. I wish I could tell you my family is finally getting over his loss. We never will.

"What is the difference between mourning and grief?" writes Roger Rosenblatt in his book *Kayak Morning* following the death of his daugh-ter. "Mourning has company."

No parent should have to endure the loss of a child. But every be-reaved parent knows through the pain, the heartache, and the loneli-ness of grief, a choice has to be made.

"A few weeks after my son was killed in an automobile accident, my wife looked at me and said, "We're going to enjoy life again. Because if we don't, our son will not be the only one who died,'" said my friend Dr. Ron Greer, who authored the book *Markings on a Windowsill: A Book About Grief That's Really About Hope.*

Somehow, someway grief is a friend, not an enemy. It's a connection and will be 'til my last breath. And that, as I have no choice but to accept, is something I'll carry forever.

I miss him. I miss him so much.

Will Garrett 2010

THE WAY

Southern Spice, *Times-Georgian,* November 1, 2015

With his heart ripped in a million pieces, Tom began his walk. After hearing the news of his son Danny's tragic death while exploring the Camino de Santiago trail through the Pyrenees Mountains in Spain, he felt called to finish his son's journey.

As an ophthalmologist who took care of others, Tom canceled all of his appointments for the next two months. His grief called him overseas. He needed to care for himself before he could once again care for others.

When he arrived in Spain, a man handed Tom a box containing his son's ashes. Tom knew what he had to do.

"I'm going to walk the Camino de Santiago," said Tom, referring to the spiritual journey that pilgrims of all faiths and backgrounds have traversed for centuries to the supposed burial spot of the apostle St. James.

"Tom, if you'll pardon me, please, you are not prepared to go on this trip," said the man somewhat taken aback. "You have no equipment, or..."

"I've got Danny's backpack and all his stuff," said Tom cutting the man off.

"But you haven't trained for this walk, and, no disrespect, you are more than sixty years old," said the man.

"So it'll take me a bit longer than most," Tom shrugs.

"You'll be lucky if you finish in two months," said the man.

"Well, then I'd better get started," said Tom. "We're leaving in the morning."

"We," replied the man looking a bit confused.

"Both of us," said Tom while holding up the box of his son's ashes.

And so begins the story of Tom's grief after his profound loss in the 2011 movie *The Way*.

"The whole journey is about showing our brokenness," said actor Martin Sheen, who portrayed Tom in the film. "It's about opening up and being human. And that's what spirituality really is. It's humanity."

More than a thousand days have passed since my family lost Will. We buried him on November 1, three years ago on All Saints' Day, a time where the church honors all of those who have walked on this earth and are no longer with us.

Grief is brutally painful.

"It's important to give your grief a voice," said counselor and author Dr. Ron Greer. "Whether it's crying it out, writing it out, walking it out, talking it out—one has to get it out. Every person has to discover his or her way and to feel the grief. They need to get in touch with their tears.

"Go to the cemetery, get out the family albums, and let the tears flow and flow," continued Greer, who lost a son more than thirty years ago. "Suppression brings depression. Expression brings resurrection, a new emotional life so that we experience a new day and begin to experience life again."

Every now and then, something or someone appears at the right time. Recently, while having a difficult day, I turned on my television and watched the end of the Disney animation movie *Up*. The main character is a cranky old man who becomes lost in grief from losing his wife of many years.

After scrolling through a scrapbook full of memories, he discovers a handwritten note from his late spouse stuck between the pages. It was a message of hope. In some ways, the message was directed at me as well. It was as if I heard my son Will's voice whisper when I read the words:

"Thanks for the adventure—now go have a new one."

The Garretts in Yosemite National Park 2015

Henry (left), Charlie (middle) and Joe at Niagra Falls 2016

The Garretts at Montmorency Falls in Quebec City, Canada 2016

EPILOGUE

MUST BE AN OMEN

Southern Spice, *Times-Georgian*, August 16, 2015

———

G rasshoppers can only jump forward.

For most of my life, I've only thought of these tiny green insects as making a crackling sound to Mother Nature's music. But recently one appeared inside my house above my back door to teach me something new.

It all started with a dog—and a teenager.

Last week, my oldest son Turner turned thirteen years old. It's an exciting time to watch him enter a new phase of independence, self-discovery, raging hormones, and eventually pimples on the front of his nose. His adolescent years will hopefully be filled with many great memories and joyous moments. But as anyone who's ever raised a teenager knows—it won't be easy.

"Even as kids reach adolescence, they need more than ever for us to watch over them," said child-rearing expert and acclaimed author Dr. Ron Taffel. "Adolescence is not about letting go. It's about hanging on during a very bumpy ride."

The seasons come and go. Somewhere along the way, even in the darkest of times, an angel appears without wings. In Turner's case, an angel appeared in a cage wagging his tail.

His grandparents surprised him with an eight-week-old puppy. In fact, my entire family was surprised.

"I thought you said you bought him a new watch," my wife said, with a smile to her mother.

"Surprise," her mom replied grinning ear to ear.

My family quickly fell in love with the new dog. And like having a new child in the home, we know the future will clearly be different with the new addition.

The first night, the puppy slept great and even used the potty in our backyard, when we took him outside. As the morning coffee brewed in the kitchen, and the dog chewed on a toy, my wife called me into the kitchen to inform me we had a visitor.

"A couple of hours ago, a grasshopper was sitting above our back door," she said. "I picked it up and threw it outside. And now another grasshopper is back sitting in the exact same spot. I hope it's not a bad omen."

She decided to research the significance of a grasshopper appearing inside a home.

According to many beliefs and cultures, a grasshopper in the house represents good luck. It often symbolizes you are about to take a giant leap of faith to change a specific area in your life without fear. It also could be telling you to go ahead and move forward, getting past what is hindering you.

For the most part, all possible outcomes will be positive.

Furthermore, for almost three years I feel as though I'm treading in grief since losing my son. There are too many days where I'm so damn tired of feeling sad, I want to feel normal, laugh, and erase the tragedy from my mind.

It's often too heavy. And then something comes along and lightens the load.

Maybe the grasshopper happened to get lost and found a way into my home last Sunday morning. But I don't think it was an accident.

Grasshoppers can only move forward, not sideways or backwards.

And maybe the little insect arrived as a small messenger from another world to teach me this lesson. I haven't seen an angel, only a grasshopper. But I feel as though this tiny little creature, along with a new puppy and a teenager, are leading the way.

Turner and his dog Teddy 2015

ACKNOWLEDGEMENTS

———

I was an average student.

Writing was somewhat of a chore because my teachers wanted me to learn how to spell, diagram sentences, write research papers and five paragraph essays as preparation for college. In hindsight, I'm glad they did, and I'm forever grateful to my outstanding elementary and middle school English teachers Pat Conerly, Virginia Busby, Diane Rooks, Alan Krieger, Marilyn Coulon, and the late Beverly Goodwin. Thank you all for teaching me the foundation of good writing skills.

It wasn't until my senior year of high school when my English teacher Mike Entrekin gave our class a creative writing assignment that I realized I actually loved writing.

When Mr. Entrekin passed out the graded papers, he told me I had a gift and encouraged me to become a writer. A few days later, he died of a heart attack.

"If you'll be yourself and write from the heart, you can never go wrong," said Entrekin.

It's amazing how one person's encouragement or one school assignment can change someone. Mr. Entrekin's words inspired me to join my high school newspaper staff *The Gold & Black* which led me to work with former West Georgia College Sports Information Director Dan Minish, who volunteered his time to teach me the basics of journalism. Thanks, Dan.

When I was a student at the University of Georgia, I handled public relations for the men's tennis team in the UGA Sports Information Department, guided by the late Dan Magill, wrote feature stories for *Georgia Bulldog Magazine,* delivered radio sports reports on WRFC, and occasionally had pieces published in the *Athens Banner-Herald,* under the tutelage of some of the best writers and broadcasters in the business: Claude Felton, Mark Parkman, Tim Hicks, Mike Mobley, Jack Calhoun, Karleen Lawrence, Wendi McLendon-Pruett, Ben May, Jeff Hundley, Graham Edwards, Scott Howard, and the late Norm Reilly.

After I graduated, I decided to take a break for twenty years from journalism.

Unfortunately, it would take a funeral to bring me back.

When *Times-Georgian* columnist Carol Martin died in January 2012, I felt called to write a story about her while sitting on the back row of the Carrollton First United Methodist Church during her service. Carol was a dear friend, and I spent hours in her front yard playing baseball and football as a child.

Thankfully, former publisher Leonard Woolsey and *Times-Georgian* editor Bruce Browning decided to publish my story about Carol.

It takes a team to write a weekly column. Tyler Sabo is the absolute best editor in journalism today. He challenges every sentence, choice of words, and punctuation with the keenest eye. It was Tyler who pushed me to leave my office and drive to the *Times-Georgian* without an appointment on a cold January day in 2012. Woolsey could have easily said "no," but instead he encouraged me to submit more columns.

I'm still submitting them.

My wife Ali edits the final draft with the diligence and insight of a great English teacher. Thank you for helping me meet all deadlines. I haven't been late yet.

Furthermore, I give special thanks to:

My coworkers: Clay Robinson, Frank Deems, Alison Wallace, and Paula Swinson, who through the years have stopped for a few minutes during their busy schedules to offer quality feedback before submitting some of these writings to publish.

My clergy friends: The Very Reverend Hazel Glover and Dr. Steve Davis for encouraging me to keep writing through the pain of losing my son.

My reading mentor: the late Dr. Ferrell Drummond, who expanded my intellectual capacity from reading only Lewis Grizzard books to experiencing the great novelists Fitzgerald, Steinbeck, Tolstoy, Pat Conroy, and John Irving.

My storytelling mentors: Mike Steed, who tells me when I use the words "that" and "just" too much; Dave Sheinin, who provides encouragement for me to continue stacking paragraphs so he can keep up with the news back home while sitting in his office at the *Washington Post*; and Ron Greer, who knows what it's like to lose a son and has encouraged me to write about grief and "get it out," instead of suppressing it.

My spiritual mentors: Joyce Alford, who "dared me to be different"; Terry Lowry, who keeps rhythm in my life by teaching me every Friday morning to hit the right keys on the piano with heart and soul; and the late Brother Jim Rains and my cohorts from working during the summer months at Noah's Ark in Panama City Beach, Florida for sparking me on this never-ending, ever-evolving spiritual journey.

To my extended family who grew up in the Chapel Heights subdivision, including Sam "Big T" Haney, Joe "Pugs" Murrah, Charlie Murrah, Scott Martin, the Muse boys, the Duffeys, the Bradys, the Musselwhites, the Comanecis and Big A—thanks for the good times.

To Matt Carter, David Hughes, and Phillip Wiggins—well done for contributing as "local experts," "storytellers" and "pundits" for the content of so many columns.

I lift up with enormous gratitude to my small group of friends who have counseled with me following my family's tragedy: Aunt Edith Yates, Scott Barrett, Wayne and Jeri Garner, Beverly Kaiser, Sue Brand, Don and Sylvia Shaw, Bobby Lovvorn and Mary Nell Lovvorn—we will always share a bond and know the darkness from losing a child.

I give a special thanks to Mike Lively for his daily texts for 365 days following Will's death, and Bill and Julie Parrish for walking side by side with my family through difficult days. Thank you all for giving my family hope in the darkest moments.

It's been said, "Family is where life begins and love never ends." I'm forever grateful for my parents Jimmy and Betty Garrett for their wonderful guidance, support and giving me so much material to write about from our crazy household. My brothers Bob and Bill have brought more laughter into my life than anyone else and I'm grateful for all of our fun times together and their beautiful families.

Special thanks to my wife's parents Randy and Lynde Turner and my wife's gorgeous sisters for always making life and each family gathering so much fun. Also, thanks to my brothers-in-laws, Eric McLendon and David Stark, for being heroes to my son Will.

I will forever be indebted to my church family at St. Margaret's Episcopal Church in Carrollton, Georgia for truly loving and supporting my family unconditionally through our tragedy. And to my extended family from Houma, Louisiana: the Starks, the Webbs, the Domangues, the Weisheits—thank you for bringing music into my life.

Most of all, I thank God for my family who has given me life's most enormous joy. My wife Ali is my best friend, the mother of my children and the strongest woman I know. The bond between a mother and child is like no other and Ali has held our family together through this difficult journey. I love you Ali and can't imagine my life without you.

My children Turner, Charlie and Henry bring so much fun, laughter, and love into our household. Everyday is a joy to spend with each of you. You all are so intelligent, possess incredible wit and wisdom—and your never-ending curiousity, deep empathy for others and love of exploring new things will serve you all well in the years ahead. Thank you all for enduring my crazy stories and for letting me sing you a song before you fall asleep. I'm so proud of each of you, and I love you all more than you'll ever know.

To my son Will, your short time on earth brought our family a profound sense of unconditional love and joy. Our hearts will forever ache from your absence until we see you again.

Finally, thanks to my audience. My stories are designed to hopefully help my readers pause and reflect on life's simple pleasures outside of the day to day news stories filled with political jargon and crimes. Hopefully, some of these stories have made your lives a little better.

Even if you didn't grow up in Carrollton, Georgia, maybe you'll find yourself in some of my stories. You are more than an audience. You are my friends.

ABOUT THE AUTHOR

———

Joe Garrett writes a weekly Sunday column for the *Times-Georgian's* Southern Spice section and is a contributing writer to *West Georgia Living* magazine. His column has been given three awards by the Georgia Press Association, including the Joe Parham Trophy in the humorous column category and the Otis A. Brumby Trophy in the serious column category.

Garrett graduated from the University of Georgia's Grady College of Journalism and Mass Communication. He specialized in studying public relations and business.

In addition to writing, Garrett works as a financial advisor as head of Garrett & Robinson Investment Management & Wealth Planning. *Atlanta Magazine* named him a five-star wealth manager, and the *Times-Georgian* has named his firm best financial advisor/planner four times.

Garrett lives with his wife, Ali, and their sons in Carrollton, Georgia.

The Garrett family 2015

In 2014, the City of Carrollton City Council named the stage at The AMP in honor of Will. Since 2013, the Garrett family and the band Baby Bee have held an annual concert in Will's memory.